To Eugene

Enjoy the book Mate

A True Story

The Akiens Steeple Jacks

of

Bel Grave, Leicester.

By

Scott Paul Akiens

For my Kids, my Dad, the whole family both past & present, and the good people of Belgrave & Leicester.

©Scott Paul Akiens Publishing 2020

FIRST EDITION

ISBN : 9781527272811

This book contains occasional moderate bad language, a bit of humour, some old fashioned violence, one or two home truths, a splash of blasphemy, and tonnes of history.

The website that accompanies this book is under construction but it gives you some idea of this books content.

www.the-akiens-steeplejacks.com

A true story, about a family who did some of the most dangerous, brutally punishing and important work you could find. For over 300 years, throughout the industrial revolution, generations of the Akiens family were *SteepleJacks.*

They built, demolished and repaired the huge Victorian factory chimneys and the centuries old church steeples, sometimes after they`d been struck by bolts of lightning. From the moment they could walk, both the boys and the girls climbed, the whole family went up these massive structures.

They fearlessly stood on the tops of massive burning chimney stacks hundreds of feet up, knocking them down brick by brick using sledge hammers and pick axes. They worked in all weathers, without any safety at all. The Akiens were famous all over the country for the work they did and were widely regarded as the best steeplejack family in England.

They had quite a reputation for being a rough, hard family, well known for getting into trouble. If you lived in Belgrave in Leicester a century ago, you more than probably knew them. There were quite a few Akiens`s living in Belgrave back then, or Dummy Town as it was also known. Most of them were steeplejacks. My Dad was the last, in our line.

They were in the papers a fair bit a hundred years ago for all sorts of reasons. Mostly for their work, sometimes for their charity work, court cases, breaking world records, meeting royalty, terrible accidents, family disputes, assault charges, war heroics, poisoning allegations, saving people`s lives, sadly getting killed, miraculous escapes and acts of bravery. You don't have to take my word for any of it, its all in the newspapers you are about to read, that were printed years before I was born.

The work they did on the factory chimneys was very important, they kept the foundry's, the potteries, the breweries, the cotton mills, the hosiery and shoe factories operational, so people could work and feed their families, pay their rents and keep their homes warm. This was at a time when most of the everyday things people needed to live, were made in England.

If the factories couldn't run because they had no power, people didn't work, they didn't get paid. There was no social security to fall back on, people, sometimes whole families, ended up in the workhouse. The steeplejacks work enabled communities to prosper, without it, people went hungry. People couldn't work in factories where the chimney could fall through the roof at any moment. Something that happened too often, a lot of people were killed.

Throughout the industrial revolution and numerous wars, they repaired the chimneys that were very often either cracked clean through high up by bolts of lightning, thick with soot billowing out toxic sulphur fumes, or they were very, very, big. Sometimes they were all three. However badly cracked they were, however much they rocked, however filthy, or however big they were, they took them all on. They never ever turned a job down because it was dangerous. They didn`t have hard hats, gloves, goggles or steel toe capped boots, no pneumatic drills or power tools at all, and without any safety lines what so ever. They didn`t have thermals or waterproofs, they went off to work in suits, shirts, ties, and a cloth cap.

Without people willing to do the work my family and other steeplejacks did, England would never have been the superpower it was at that time. They kept the big home fires burning that fuelled the industrial revolution. No other superpower in history has ever ruled over as much of the world as the British empire did at that time. Over 70 of the countries on todays map of the world. India, Africa, North America, Canada, Australia to name a few.

Their work helped enable the factories of the war machine to stay in production, those that helped keep us from losing the wars. Steeplejacks did more than their bit for the country, for a very long time. From as far afield as Cornwall to Glasgow, the family worked on many jobs that no one else would take on. Fair play to anyones families who were awarded wartime medals for bravery, they should be very proud. Just as i am for all the acts of bravery my family did, during both war and peace time.

When you see all the times they were in the newspapers, and what was written about them, it gives you some idea of just how well known they were back then. It`s fair to say you don`t find many families with histories like this very often. Although im sure there are loads of families with colourful histories out there, just waiting to have their stories told by their family today. Most of my family today know they come from the steeplejacks, but they probably don`t know much more than that. They don't realise just how dangerous it was, or

4

what the job entailed. Those distant relatives in the family that have contacted me from different parts of the world who have seen the website, had no idea their history was so colourful. Until i started researching it, neither did i.

When i was researching all the family history stuff online, i came across loads of things about them. It gutted me a bit that both Dad and Granddad have passed away, they would`ve loved to have seen them all. To clarify they weren`t bullshitting about the stories they told me, if nothing else. There were hundreds of articles written about them, so i thought id build a website and stick it all on there. So the rest of the family all over the world can see it, this is their history too. Any Belgrave / Leicester people who might remember them, or anyone else who might just find this insight into steeplejacks lives in general, or the families history interesting. Initially my main reason for writing this was for my kids, because there is so much they don't know, and also the rest of the family, so they can find out about where they come from. Then I thought i,may as well make it into a book, there`s certainly enough stuff to go in it. It won`t be everyone`s cup of tea naturally, especially anyone who`s squeamish, some of it is pretty brutal at times. Its not my intention to shock people or to glorify some of the things i grew up hearing about the family, im just writing the stories as i was told them. It probably won`t be for anyone who`s averse to the odd bit of moderate bad language either.

I left school without any qualifications at all, so i don`t expect this book to win any literary awards, i couldn`t give a toss to be honest, i didn`t write it for the sort of people "qualified" to judge it in that way. You don`t need any of those qualifications, you just need people telling your families stories and someone else to write it all down. I`d sooner this gave ordinary people a few ideas and maybe help to inspire them to write theirs. They say everyone has a book or two in them, you`re families history ought to be one of them. I`m not bothered if the punctuation isn`t up to scratch, there`s the odd spelling mistake, if iv repeated myself from time to time, or if its not all in the right order. Im not bothered if it doesn't make a few quid, I`m just happy to tell the story. Iv purposely put a little bit about my Dads death at the beginning of this because I don't want it to end on a sad note, and he certainly wouldn't either.

Iv never written a book before so this is all new. Iv written it in a way, that i think the family of the past, and hopefully the present, would probably have wanted it written, with no heirs or graces. Which is why im not having any of it proof read or edited by anyone, other than family with stories to add. We`ve always done things our own way. Im not adding an about the author page, instead iv put a few of my stories in it here and there, not steeplejack related.

Dad was given a copy of the family tree a few months before he died. That's what started all this. He thought it would make an interesting read if all the stories about some of the characters in the family over the years were put together. He wanted them to be more than just another name on the family tree. He was very proud of what he and the family before him did, what his cousins, uncles and aunts did. Visiting relatives, some of the Akiens from up north travelled from over 200 miles away, to come and say goodbye. They`d heard about his illness being terminal and expected the visit to be a sad one. He made them laugh the whole time they were there. My cousin told me, they were amazed by him, because he was in such good spirits. He was so pleased they came to see him. He didn't want them leaving feeling sad. If they hadn't given him that copy of the family tree, you wouldn't be reading this now.

We must have both read that family tree a dozen times over the coming months until he passed away. He would go through the names of his uncles and aunts in Granddads generation, and their kids, his cousins, telling me different stories he knew about some of them. Its not my place to write about them so im not going to. That's up to them if they`d like me to add any of their stories to the revised edition of this book. Dad knew he wouldn't be around to tell his grandkids himself, because he was dying of terminal bone cancer. That saddened him more than anything, knowing he would never know them. It was probably the only thing that saddened him to be honest. You wouldn't believe the laughs we had on his death bed during those last 6 months of his life. He laughed even through all that pain and knowing he was dying.

Knowing dad he would want this book to be a few things. He would want it to be as true (as possible), down to earth for ordinary working class people, but probably more importantly, he would want it to hopefully give people a few laughs. So iv added a few stories I remember that made us both laugh over the years, later on in the book. There will be more in the next book im sure. There`s been enough dark times, hardship and heartache, since they very first began climbing the chimneys and steeples, centuries ago. As you are about to read. Not all of the newspaper articles iv used are about the family.

I was told so many stories about the family growing up. I didn't have to go through what dad, granddad and all those others in the generations before them did. I was lucky, in some ways, I went to work inside a factory. The one I went in was a right shit hole. The health and safety was probably better in Victorian times. Im the first generation in 300 years not to climb. Writing about what they all did just seems like the next best thing to me. There's too much history to let it just get forgotten. I'm proud of them for what they did, just like people are rightfully proud of their families for being war heroes, firemen, nurses, miners or whatever. Miners had probably an equally tough, dangerous working life to those of steeplejacks. One had the worry of the ground falling in crushing them to death, the other had the worry of falling to their deaths on the ground. The two were at opposite ends of the industrial revolution process. Miners mined the coal deep underground that was needed for the steam powered engines, steeplejacks dealt with the outcome of all that at the top of the chimneys.

Back in the old days the family went everywhere by horse and cart. The whole family would set off from their terraced house in Belgrave, Leicester, early in the freezing cold mornings, to go and repair a chimney or a church steeple somewhere in the country. Just getting there would have been a job and a half, travelling for days in some cases, sleeping rough in fields along the way. The cart would be stacked high with ladders, ropes, work tools, all the children, and both parents. Even their wives got stuck in. Great grandma had no problem going up the ladders, she worked with her husband on a lot of jobs.

A 310 feet-high chimney-stack, said to be the second tallest in Britain——is being demolished. The wife of the steeplejack is helping with the work.

A 310 feet high chimney stack, said to be the second tallest in Britain-- is being demolished. The wife of the steeplejack is helping with the work.

****

7

In the next newspaper photos, all of the younger ones are wearing the safety belts. They were fearless of the heights and worked as if they were on the ground as the newspapers reported, because of the early introduction to heights. It`s unimaginable in this day and age, how anyone could send their kids up these things, but they did. But then it`s also unimaginable, that people would send their 5 year old kids into factories, to work 14 hours a day, 6 days a week. Life was very hard all round for all our families back in them days.

A Remarkable Family of Steeplejacks.

Miss Lydia Aiken, aged 15, who is a member of a family of steeplejacks living in Newington street, Leicester, last week performed a remarkable feat there by scaling two chimney shafts over 150ft. high. Her ascent was accomplished in five minutes, the descent in four. Miss Aiken now challenges every girl under 18 to a steeple or chimney climbing competition. Her father, Mr. J. T. Aiken, and his ancestors for 200 years have been professional climbers, and he is bringing up his family in the same way. He is also an active member of the Leicester Ambulance Brigade, and his three boys are trained in fire-escape and ambulance work. Miss Lydia Aiken and her father will next Wednesday ascend and inspect a tall chimney at St. Helens, damaged in one of the recent thunderstorms. The top right hand picture shows Mr. Aiken training his boys. The left hand picture is one of Mr. Aiken and his sons on the top stage of a shaft. The little lad standing out in a perilous position is the five year old Alfred, who climbed without assistance. In the family group the names, reading from left to right, are:—(1) Mr. J. T. Aiken, jun., age 20. (2) Master Jesse Aiken, age 11. 3. Master Alfred Fredk. Baden Aiken, age 5. (4) Miss Lydia Aiken, age 15. (5) Master Harold Aiken, age 9. (6) Mr. J. T. Aiken, sen., the father of the family.

A Remarkable Family of Steeplejacks

Miss Lydia Akiens, aged 15, who is a member of a family of steeplejacks living in Newington street, Leicester, last week performed a remarkable feat

8

there by scaling two chimney shafts over 150 ft. high. Her ascent was accomplished in five minutes, the descent in four. Miss Akiens now challenges every girl under 18 to a steeple or chimney climbing competition.

Her father, Mr. J. T. Akiens, and his ancestors for 200 years have been professional climbers, and he is bringing up his family in the same way. He is also an active member of the Leicester Ambulance Brigade, and his three boys are trained in fire-escape and ambulance work. Miss Lydia Akiens and her father will next Wednesday ascend and inspect tall chimney St. Helens, damaged in one of the recent thunderstorms.

The top right hand picture shows Mr. Akiens training his boys. The left hand picture is one of Mr. Akiens and his sons on the top stage of shaft. The little lad standing out in a perilous position is the 5 year old Alfred, who climbed without assistance. In the family group the names, reading from left to right, are:—(l) Mr. J. T. Akiens, jun., age 20. (2) Master Jesse Akiens, age 11. (3). Master Alfred Frederick Baden Akiens, age 5. (4) Miss Lydia Akiens, age 15. (5) Master Harold Akiens, age 9. (6) Mr. J. T. Akiens, is the father of the family.

****

Steeplejacks possibly did the worst and most dangerous work the industrial revolution and the churches of England needed doing. The Akiens steeplejacks did some of the very worst, of the worst work, that other steeplejacks couldn't or wouldn't do, what they were afraid to do. The family did the dirty work, as they called it.

Sometimes they would be going off to repair something somewhere in the country that was especially dangerous, something that the local steeplejacks wouldn't go near. They could see their days work before they got to it, a big broken chimney or steeple in the distance, the damage becoming more and more clearer the closer they got.

The family chose to work above these death trap factories instead of in them. They couldn`t "drop" most of these chimneys in the usual way in these built up areas, because the factories still needed them back then. So they had to be taken down the hardest way, one brick at a time. Before any "experts" think, that`s not how it was done, id like to point out it`s not something iv ever done, i wasn`t a steeplejack, im going from memory of what i was told years ago.

A typical view from the sort of places where they worked high up.

Towns and cities back then were dirty smog filled places, people lived in extreme poverty. Thousands of people died because of respiratory problems due to the smog and fumes. The chimneys were built so big for two reasons. To expel the fumes high up away from people`s houses and the factories, and also to obtain a hotter draught for the furnaces.

Factories were very dangerous places in those days, little or no health and safety existed. Children were forced to work in these death trap factories, thousands of them were badly injured and many were killed doing dangerous jobs. When they got injured in factories losing fingers or limbs in machinery, wages were stopped from the instant the accident happened, they received no medical assistance however serious the injury, they received no compensation and were discarded as being useless. Children had very hard lives back then, the kids in our family just had a different kind of hard life. Child labour contributed massively to the wealth of Victorian England. The sort of dangers they faced working in these factories was best evidenced in the 1828 Memoir of Robert Blincoe by John Brown.

In the memoir he recounts witnessing a scene of horror.

"A girl named Mary Richards, who was thought remarkably pretty when she left the workhouse, and, who was not quite ten years of age, attended a drawing frame, below which, and about a foot from the floor, was a horizontal shaft, by which the frames above were turned. It happened one evening, when her apron was caught by the shaft. In an instant the poor girl was drawn by an irresistible force and dashed on the floor. She uttered the most heart-rending shrieks!

The factory overseer ran towards her, an agonized and helpless beholder of a scene of horror. He saw her whirled round and round with the shaft - he heard the bones of her arms, legs, thighs, etc. successively snap asunder, crushed, seemingly, to atoms, as the machinery whirled her round, and drew tighter and tighter her body within the works, her blood was scattered over the frame and streamed upon the floor, her head appeared dashed to pieces. At last, her mangled body was jammed in so fast, between the shafts and the floor, that the water being low and the wheels off the gear, it stopped the main shaft. When she was extricated, every bone was found broken - her head dreadfully crushed. She was carried off quite lifeless." These types of situations occurred because children were given clothing that did not fit. Also, they were sometimes required to operate machines without any protection at all, such as shoes."

****

11

The next article from 1871 was written about my great grt grt uncle Samuel. He suffered a very horrific death after being dragged through a wood plaining machine. His sleeve got caught in the drive belts. His injuries were shocking, such an awful way to die.

FATAL ACCIDENT.-

On Wednesday last, an inquest was held on the body of Samuel Akiens, before J. Gregory,Esq. (Borough Coroner), at the George and Dragon Inn, Kent Street, Infirmary-square.- Mr. W. Flowers, house-surgeon at the Infirmary, said deceased was admitted on Tuesday morning about Ten o`clock, and he found him suffering from a dislocation of both knees, and the right ankle, with fracture of the right fibula, and one of the bones of the left arm.

There were also several ribs on both sides fractured, and there were cuts and bruises nearly over the whole body. He was cold and collapsed, and died in about an hour from general shock caused by the injuries.- Ephraim Bell said he was a sawyer employed at the workshops of Messrs.

12

Neale and Son in Peacock-lane, and deceased worked a plaining machine at the same place. The machinery was worked by steam. On Tuesday morning, between nine and ten o`clock, deceased said to him, " I want to grind but the belt is off ; I will fetch a lace to lace it."

He then went out of the shop below, and he (witness) did not see him again until he heard a noise in the shop or shed below, and went down with several others and found him in a sort of recess or corner of the shed, where the belt drives from. Deceased was on the floor with his clothes partly torn off, and was in a speechless and insensible state. He was brought out, and a doctor was sent for who came and saw him, and after that was taken to the Infirmary. His (Witness`s) belief was that the shaft had caught his loose jacket, and dragged him and whirled him round by it till his clothes gave way, and he fell.- Some corroborative evidence was given, and a verdict of "accidental death" was returned.

****

When they went to work on these rotten or broken chimneys, they began by chiselling a hole into the brickwork, at the base of the chimney and then hammered a wooden peg into it. Then they hammered an iron dog into the wooden peg, like a primitive raw plug. A dog is an iron spike about 10 inches long, with a hook on the end. Then they lashed a ladder to it and would then climb up that ladder secured only at the bottom, to knock another dog into the chimney wall so they could secure the ladder at the top. Once secured at the top and bottom, they would climb to the top of the ladder, throw one leg over the top rung and hook their foot under the second rung, so they could stretch up as high as they could to chisel out another hole for the next wooden peg and dog, a few feet higher up for the lower part of the next ladder.

That would be scary enough at the top of just one ladder for many people, let alone 20, 30 or 40 ladders up a chimney in the high winds. The winds up there are a lot stronger and colder than they are down on the ground. The chimneys sway from side to side as much as a foot or more, at the top of the really big ones. It felt like they were onboard a ship at times.

The next 16 foot heavy ladder would be carried up on their shoulder and tied to the first ladder, overlapping it by half its length, so they could climb up to knock in the second dog for that ladder. Then they would untie the overlapping ladder and slide it up in place, so it could be tied to both dogs making the ladder safe at the top and the bottom. The process would be repeated to make one continuous ladder going all the way up.

Each time a new ladder was needed one of them would make the climb down to fetch another, sometimes they would carry two up, one on each shoulder to save time. It was exhausting work just getting the chimneys laddered. When dad and granddad worked together it was always dad who fetched the ladders, he was younger and could climb faster. At some point on some of the chimneys, they would have to pass a crack going down it, or right through it, after it had been hit by a bolt of lightning. On the majority of these jobs it was possible to fix steel bands round the chimneys to support them. Some were too badly damaged for that and had to be demolished.

Beyond the point where it was cracked, the work became extremely dangerous. Sometimes the whole chimney stack rocked on that crack, as they made their way up to the top. At any moment they could all come crashing down with hundreds of tonnes of masonry around them. Like it nearly did when Five of them were working on this chimney written about below, the widest in Leicestershire. The article in full is further on in the book.

ence he had at Thurcaston whilst repairing the widest chimney in Leicestershire. The top of the chimney was very badly cracked, and whilst working at a height of 150 feet the party, which numbered five, became conscious that ten tons of masonry had shifted, and threatened to topple over at any moment, bringing death and disaster to them all. The only way of saving their lives was

As they got near the top there would sometimes be an overhang like the one pictured below, which was usually 2 or 3 feet but could be as much as 7 or 8 feet. This was the most dangerous part of the climb. The ladders could be at a 45 degree angle to the chimney, with nothing between them and the ground but a very strong grip.

Once they reached the top the hard graft began dismantling the thing. First they would use pulleys to lower down any heavy, decorative carved coping stones by rope, ready for when they were put back. Then they took the chimneys down brick by brick swinging pick axes and sledge hammers, standing on just the broken rotting chimney walls and 9 inch scaffold boards spanning the top. Once they reached the crack, they built them back up as good as new. Sometimes they worked in the rain, sometimes they went up with ice on the ladders. That sort of work took balls.

Victorian England was a very different place to the world we live in today. Long before central heating, double glazed windows, and all those other modern luxuries we take for granted today. They didn`t even have running water, just a shared water pump in the yard. Up to a dozen families would share a single outside toilet. You had a luke warm or cold bath, which was a tin tub in the back yard. If you were lucky, the water was hot and you had it in front of the coal fire.

The tightly packed houses were cold, draughty, damp, overcrowded places to live, they were slums. The house i was born in on Evans street in Belgrave was a slum. The windows were falling out, the walls were crumbling, it was damp and freezing cold. I was a very sickly baby, I couldn't keep any food down, the house made me ill. Mam and Dad didn't expect me to live, they thought id died a few times. He kept my cot at the side of his bed. When we moved out of Belgrave across the river to stocking farm my health picked up immediately. It was demolished in the slum clearance programs in the 60`s and 70`s in Leicester shortly after we left and moved to Stocking Farm. No electricity or gas, they lived by candlelight or paraffin lamps. 5 or 6 children sharing one bed was common in big families. Below is a photo of the back of the houses on Evans street Belgrave, the sort of place many people lived in back then. We have no idea how lucky we are these days.

Disease was rife, partly because of the poor sanitation, partly because of all the smog, poor diet, and a lack of medicine. My aunt remembers that if anyone in the family caught T.B, a shed would be used to house them at the bottom of the garden, until they died. My Great granddad and two of the children on my grandmas side all died from T.B. Child mortality rates were pitiful, only about half of all children made it to their 5th birthdays. Granddad had two siblings he never met, they died before he was born. The article below is about one of his elder sisters, Florence but she was remembered as Beaty, her middle name was Beatrice. She may have had a twin sister, Sarah Ellen Akiens, named after great grandma. She died aged just two weeks old.

16

DEATH FROM SUFFOCATION.—An inquest was held by Mr. Robert Harvey, borough coroner, on Wednesday afternoon at the Catherine-street Board Schools, on the body of Florence Beatrice Akiens, aged 14 days, child of John Thomas and Ellen Akiens, 113, Belper-street. According to the evidence of the mother the child was healthy, and was taken to bed with its mother and father on Monday night apparently all right. It lay between its parents on its mother's arm, and just after seven the next morning was found by the mother lying dead in the same position as when she went to sleep. —Dr. Lewitt, who was called in, attributed death to suffocation from overlaying.—Witness added that although he was afraid the practice of allowing the child to lie on the mother's arm with its head against the breast was very prevalent it was extremely risky. A verdict of accidental death was returned.

LEICESTER LIBERAL ASSOCIATION.—A meeting of

DEATH FROM SUFFOCATION -

An inquest was held by Dr. Robert Harvey, Borough Coroner on Wednesday afternoon at the Catherine street board schools, on the body of Florence Beatrice Akiens, Daughter of John Thomas Akiens and Ellen Akiens, 113 Belper street. According to the evidence of the mother the child was healthy, and was taken to bed with its mother and father on Monday night apparently all right. It lay between its parents on its mothers arm, and just after seven the next morning was found by the mother lying dead in the same position as when she went to sleep. Dr. Lewitt, who was called in, attributed death to suffocation from overlaying. Witness added that although he was afraid the practise of allowing the child to lie on its mothers arm with its head against the breast was very prevalent, it was extremely risky. A verdict of accidental death was returned.

****

17

Below is a page from the family tree that gives you some idea how awful things were back then.

To give you some idea of how the poor people lived and died in the 1600's and 1700's, an entry from the vicar of St. Margaret's, Belgrave, Leicester, dated October 1710 reads:

'buried boy, name unknown, 5 years old, found in The Newarks, Leicester.'

Another entry, dated December 1870:

'dead baby, brought to vicarage by girl, father unknown soldier, mother's name not given.'

A lot of your relatives, most from large families, died either at birth or at a young age, due to lack of medicine and food, and living in damp, cold houses.

To give you some idea how the poor people lived and died in the 1600`s and 1700`s, an entry from the vicar of St Margarets, Belgrave, Leicester, dated October 1710 reads,: Buried boy, name unknown, 5 years old, found in the Newarks, Leicester.

Another entry dated December 1870 :

Dead baby bought to vicarage by girl, father unknown soldier, mothers name not given.

A lot of your relatives, most from large families died either at birth or a young age, due to lack of medicine, food, and living in damp, cold houses.

****

Those children that were lucky enough to survive those early years, soon went off to work in factories, mines, chimneys sweeps, they did all manner of jobs that we wouldn`t dream of making our children do today, to earn a few extra pennies for the family.

Looking back to 1851, a census was carried out (always on a Sunday night). At number 15, Green Street, Leicester, lived Mrs Susanah Akins (then a widow) with Mrs Elizabeth Gastello her sister. Also there that night was William Knight, 28 years old, labourer to a bricklayer; and Knights' wife, Mary Ann, daughter of Susanah. They lived at 21, Green Street, Leicester and they had four children. Priscilla, aged seven years; William, aged five years; Rossana, aged three years and Eileen Ann, aged eight months. The two older children, Priscilla and William worked for twelve hours a day seaming yarn.

Another part of the family tree above, taken from Parish council records in 1851, tells of a Five year old and a Seven year old from one family, having to work for 12 hours a day in a factory, Five days a week. They only had to do 11 hours on Saturday and were given Sundays off. That was kind of them. Before 1833 it would have been 14 hours, the law was changed that year. If they didn't work hard enough or they complained, they'd get beaten, even horse whipped just for being late. Mill owners employed them for several reasons. They were only paid between 10% - 20% of an adults wage for doing the same work, they would be more obedient and wouldn't strike, and because they were small enough to crawl under dangerous machinery when they got jammed. Children weren't allowed to be children, they lived miserable lives. Many of these children would be plucked from the workhouses.

Poverty was so bad, they had to do what they had to do to survive, they didn't have a choice. People had very hard times, but that's how life was back in them days for a lot of people. The things our families lived through, the hardships and tragedies, we can't begin to imagine. We might have been the richest most powerful nation on earth, but we still had extreme poverty.

LEICESTER LABOUR CLUB, BELGRAVE-GATE.—The committee of the unemployed on Thursday supplied soup and bread to 300 children. The committee are in need of further funds

The newspaper articles I found online describe the steeplejacks treacherous working conditions, the sort of lives they lived, some of the risks they took and how many of them died. I've typed some of the newspaper stuff out for easier reading, some are old and the print is difficult to make out.

The article above mentions that hundreds of people came to watch them drop this brewery chimney in Exeter, and the work of felling this monster was in the hands of one of the most expert steeplejacks in the whole of England.

Taking Down a Heavitree Chimney :

OLD LANDMARK GONE

Heavitree brewery chimney

At ten minutes past four p.m, yesterday, the huge chimney of the brickyard, formerly owned by the late Mr. J. Sampson and purchased by the Exeter Brick and Tile Company and Mr. Robert Hancock- which has served for forty years as a landmark of the Priory and Polsloe Estates, suddenly tottered, swayed, and fell. At the present moment only a big trail of bricks piled up at what was once the base and extending to the deep pit at the lower end of the brickyard remains to mark the spot where it stood sentinel since 1871.

A crowd of several hundred watched it fall, they had waited from shortly after two o`clock, and the wait had been punctuated by series of thrills and false alarms. The work of felling this monster was in the hands of one of the most expert steeplejacks of England, Mr J. T. Akiens of Leicester, assisted by his younger brother.

They had hewn out the first bricks near the base on the east side early in the morning, but the business was not started in earnest until after the dinner hour."Half past two"was their prophecy for the moment of the actual collapse, but for once they were out in their reckoning. At that time the crowd of nearly a thousand people had lined up behind the iron fence of the adjacent field, and the boys of Ladysmith road school helped to swell their number, for they had been given the privilege of watching a rare sight indeed at Exeter. People too had gathered on the rising ground at the back of Polsloe road, and in fact encroached at the start almost to the base of the chimney itself. Later on however, on the advice of Mr. Hancock, who scented danger from such close proximity to the actual work, they retired some fifty yards or so further up.

Meanwhile, the two brothers dust begrimed, were hewing out the bricks one by one, or clump by clump. A gaping hole in the side of the monster was soon made, and a cane was suspended down the aperture. This cane was closely watched, for its buckling was to be the first sign of impending collapse. Three o`clock came and then half past three but no fall. Occasionally a cloud of dust went up as a cluster of bricks went down before the hammering and occasionally too, the steeple Jacks darted aside at a movement of the cane. In each instance there were shouts of "Here she comes", but they were false alarms.

The elder Akiens brother brought into play a huge crow bar, and the hole became bigger and bigger, and the steeplejacks more and more wary. The monsters fall came at last, when people were least expecting it. Only the elder brother was at work at the moment, and the first indication of what was to happen was his hurried plunge on one side. This indeed was no false alarm. The monster seemed to totter for a moment and then in a great curve fell, dividing it in the middle half way over, and the lower part collapsing while the higher half completed its quarter circle in wide sweep and pitched to the pit. A cloud of dust went up, and while people were rushing from all sides, the

Akiens stood waving their caps, and evidently well pleased that another hazardous job was over.

According to their story afterwards the chimney 130ft in height, had offered a much more difficult problem owing to its structure than they had anticipated. They had expected too that its fall would be slightly to the right, but as a matter of fact it came down almost at right angles to the end of the brickyard buildings. They have both been employed recently at work on Heavitree Church and other buildings in the neighbourhood, and yesterdays felling of the chimney is an operation which marks the closing of the brickyard.

The brothers come from a famous family of steeplejacks, and the elder one, wiry and active, could tell stories of many hairbreadth escapes. Only 2 years ago, while engaged in a contract at Sileby, he fell 80 feet and escaped serious injury by little short of a miracle. His sister Lydia Akiens is also widely known for she holds the woman`s world record in the steeplejack world.

****

Ox Tongues, Silver and Box Speciality.—Hutchings Advt. The best is cheapest.—Advt. J. T. Akiens and Sons, steeple-climbers, Leicester, are now carrying out important work in connexion with Heavitree Church, Sampson's Brickworks, and several other high structures. Mr. Akiens, junr., will be pleased to give estimates.—17, Alpha-street, Heavitree, Exeter.—Advt. Published by

When they worked away they would often work on a few structures in that area, one after another, to make the long journeys more worthwhile. There were times in the early days when they were forced to sleep rough in the open. As their situation improved they`d find digs in the town and advertise in the local papers. On this occasion they made important repairs to Heavitree church, Sampsons brick works and a few others in the Exeter area.

23

Heavitree church

Some of them fell from the tops of chimney stacks, and unbelievably survived. Granddad was one of them, he fell 3 times and lived to retirement. He was still climbing ladders doing odd jobs in his 70's. Great uncle Tom Akiens, the show off, even managed a couple of somersaults on the way down when he fell, according to this next newspaper story. He must have had very big ears is all I can think. It was miraculous that he wasn't killed. He was covered in bruises and had a dislocated shoulder. He was back at work at the top of the same chimney within four days.

STEEPLEJACKS TERRIBLE FALL AT SILEBY.

MARVELLOUS ESCAPE FROM DEATH.

A steeplejack named J.T.Akiens junior (Tom Akiens) who lives at 33 Victoria road North , Belgrave, Leicester, had a miraculous escape from instantaneous death on Tuesday afternoon at Sileby. He had been employed together with his uncle Arthur Akiens, for some time past, in repairing the chimneys at messrs, W.T. Wright and Co`s brickyard, Sileby, which is known as the Pheonix works. Yesterday afternoon he was working about 5 feet from the top of a chimney which is about 80 feet high, when he fell the entire distance to the ground.

How the accident happened no one appears to know. His uncle, who was working at the top of the chimney, only heard the cry of "oh!" and, looking down he saw his nephew, who is about 25 years of age, falling. In his descent Akiens turned a couple of somersaults, and, marvellous to relate, alighted upon his feet. Help was immediately forthcoming, and Dr Grey from Sileby, was sent for. Upon examination it was found, to the great surprise of all present, that Akiens injuries only consisted of a dislocated shoulder and a number of bad bruises.

25

After being attended at Sileby, Akiens was conveyed to Leicester by train and taken to the Infirmary. Here the house surgeon did not think it necessary to detain him in the institution, and he was afterwards taken home in a cab.

Akiens is a member of a celebrated steeplejack family, and on one occasion he ascended to the height of 440 feet. His sister Miss Lydia Akiens aged 19 years, holds the title of champion lady steeplejack, and not long ago she climbed to the top of the tower at St. Marks church, Leicester.

****

Another article that mentions Johns miraculous escape.

FALLING STARS

The art of falling great distances without serious injuries seems to be approaching perfection in this district. We had hardly got over our amazement at the comparatively safe negotiation of a sudden drop of 80 feet, on the part of John Akiens at Sileby when we were introduced to a new feat in the same direction by the two local firemen who were precipitated to the ground from alarming distances, and yet, after being taken to the infirmary, were able to proceed to their homes little worse for their alarming adventure. It is evident that if the British Aviation Society ever feels called upon to open a school to instruct air-men in the art of rapid descent, that school ought to be established in Leicester, With John Akiens as principal, and firemen Clarke and Knight as its leading professors.

****

Another time he made the papers

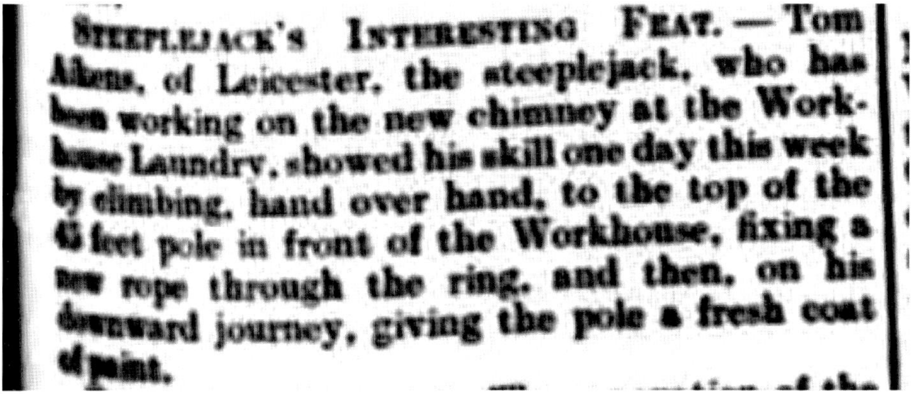

STEEPLEJACK'S INTERESTING FEAT. — Tom Akiens, of Leicester, the steeplejack, who has been working on the new chimney at the Workhouse Laundry, showed his skill one day this week by climbing, hand over hand, to the top of the 45 feet pole in front of the Workhouse, fixing a new rope through the ring, and then, on his downward journey, giving the pole a fresh coat of paint.

STEEPLEJACKS INTERESTING FEAT

Tom Akiens, of Leicester, the steeplejack who has been working on the new chimney at the workhouse laundry, showed his skill one day this week by climbing, hand over hand, to the top of the 45 feet pole in front of the workhouse, fixing a rope through a ring, and then, on his downward journey, giving the pole a fresh coat of paint.

****

Two of my great uncles, granddads brothers. John Thomas Akiens (Junior) on the left and Jesse Akiens on the right. Both would be tragically killed while they were relatively young men.

A Risky Life.

Last week Extonians by the hundred were thrilled with the work of a couple of young steeplejacks, who felled a chimney measuring 130ft, for the Exeter Brick and Tile Co. We give their photo above. On the left is Mr. J. T. Akiens, junr, and on the right Mr J Akiens, junr, both of Leicester. They are, as will be noticed, very grimy after their arduous work. Mr J T Akiens has had many thrilling escapes, and he it was who fell eighty feet from a chimney, and yet was able to resume work on the structure within four days. ("Western Times" Photo).

The above article :   1912 :

Last week Extonians by the hundreds were thrilled with the work of a couple of young steeplejacks, who felled a chimney measuring 130ft, for the exeter Brick and Tile Co. We give their photo above. On the left is Mr J. T. Akiens junr, and on the right is Mr J Akiens junr, both of Leicester. They are, as will be noticed, very grimy after their arduous work. Mr J T Akiens has had many thrilling escapes, and he it was who fell 80 feet from a chimney and yet was able to resume work on the structure within 4 days. (western times)

****

The family worked on many of the chimneys while the fires of the boilers were banked, they were still lit so production wasn`t affected as much as if the fires were completely out. When they were working on the Leicester hospital chimneys during the first world war, the clothes were burnt off their bodies. Steeplejacks were known to cook meat pies and boil potatoes, in metal buckets on the side of chimneys for their lunch, because the heat was so intense. A spark ignited one mans clothes because of the heat up there. The wooden staging would sometimes catch fire with the steeplejacks on it.

Chimneys, Mr Akiens told me, like bathroom taps, are "hot" and "cold." Often his eyebrows were singed. A chimney at a Leicestershire Colliery was so hot that woodwork erected about it by steeplejacks became ignited. A gale was blowing, and the work of those who climbed the chimney to extinguish the flames was hazardous.

****

A STEEPLEJACK IN JEOPARDY.

On Saturday last when one of those chimney climbers, known as a "steeplejack", was on the top of the stalk at Balgonie Spinning Mill, where he had been conducting some repairs, a spark from the chimney ignited his clothes, which were soon ablaze about him. In hot haste he made his descent, but not before he was scorched about the head and face, and rather severely so about the lower part of his body.

****

Pictured below, the chimney on the left is being repaired and the one on the right is being demolished.

The family would have worked on literally thousands of chimneys doing these jobs throughout their very long time in the business. Before they went on the phone they would have got a lot of their work by letters in the post. If it was an emergency and a factory or church somewhere needed their help urgently because of a lightning strike, they would receive the news via telegram.

The families advert in the Kelly`s Leicester directory. Belgrave - 61205. That was the number the vicars, the wealthy mill owners and sometimes even the government called when the families help was needed, or when they couldn`t get any other firms to do the job.

The advert from the Leicester Kelly`s directory above shows they even did the work at night, when the factories were closed for the same reason as working on the chimneys with the fires banked, so work could almost carry on as usual. Production wasn't affected so much, people`s wages weren't affected the same as if the factory had to shut down completely while they worked. A few steeplejack firms worked at night. The article below is nothing to do with the family.

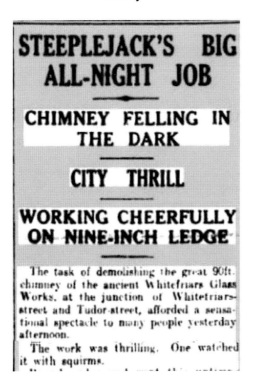

STEEPLEJACK'S BIG ALL-NIGHT JOB

CHIMNEY FELLING IN THE DARK

CITY THRILL

WORKING CHEERFULLY ON NINE-INCH LEDGE

The task of demolishing the great 90ft. chimney of the ancient Whitefriars Glass Works, at the junction of Whitefriars-street and Tudor-street, afforded a sensational spectacle to many people yesterday afternoon.

The work was thrilling. One watched it with squirms.

STEEPLEJACKS BIG ALL NIGHT JOB

CHIMNEY FELLING IN THE DARK

CITY THRILL

WORKING CHEERFULLY ON NINE INCH LEDGE

The task of demolishing the great 90 foot chimney of the ancient Whitefriars Glass Works, at the junction of Whitefriars street and Tudor street, afforded a sensational spectacle yesterday afternoon. The work was thrilling, one watched it with squirms.

Round and round went this untiring hitter, sweeping down bricks while night gathered fast. Just after seven he took a brief rest for a cup of coffee, for it is his golden rule not to eat until the work is done. A young man of 21 may do this work with impunity.

"I have never come across anything yet that i have been unable to climb".

In the dark last night, when you heard the steady tap, tap, of this human fly, as he has been called. It was uncanny. You thought of that lonely man, cheerfully swinging his heavy hammer on a nine inch ledge of brickwork, shuddered and thanked your lucky stars you were not with him.

****

They were probably as well known in the industry back then as Fred Dibnah the tv steeplejack was years later. Thousands of people came to see him take down chimneys, as many as 10,000 like when he came to Leicester on one of his programs. The family had finished their steeplejacking by this time otherwise im sure they would have got the job. Wherever they worked they always drew a big crowd of people to watch them work, never quite as many as Fred got but they didn`t have the publicity from the media he got. People were fascinated watching steeplejacks work, they always have been. To give you some idea, look at a building near you, a house or factory, maybe 30, 40 feet or a lot higher. Then imagine someone standing on the very edge of it looking down. You would not be able to take your eyes of them, its human nature. That`s why Freds popularity took off in the beginning. It was the same for the family, but long before tv came along. They were just winding up the business as he was beginning to make a name for himself.

In the early 17th century when the family first started climbing, people weren't just fascinated by steeplejacks, they were afraid of them. A time when people really believed in all that supernatural cobblers. At that time witches were still being burned at the stake. The article below -

"When you had completed your apprenticeship your learning had only just begun. To be a successful steeplejack in those days you had to be a jack of all trades. Not only an engineer but a carpenter, blacksmith, stonemason, soil expert and a structural engineer to boot."

When they were working out of town they were forced to sleep rough in the open.

||||||||||||||||||||||

"It was a common belief in those days that steeplejacks were from another world and hid their tails beneath their coats. People wouldn't have you in their houses, they thought you communed with the devil at the top of the church spire," he said.

"Believe it or not but chimneys have moods, ugly moods and happy moods. When you've been in this business as long as I have you know that to disregard these moods meant almost certain death," he added.

Not only has Mr. Akiens seen fellow workmen fall 140 feet to their death but he himself has had a number of close escapes.

||||||||||||||||||||||

"When you had finished your apprenticeship your learning had only just begun. To be a successful steeplejack in those days you had to be a jack of all trades. Not only an engineer but a carpenter, blacksmith, stonemason, soil expert and a structural engineer to boot.

When they were working out of town they were forced to sleep rough in the open.

" It was a common belief in those days, that steeplejacks were from another world and hid their tails beneath their coats and communed with the devil at the top of the church spire" he said.

****

Even up to the present century, in some parts of the country, villagers thought that steeplejacks were funny little devil men with horns and a tail. So deep rooted was the suspicion that parents would keep their children indoors until they got to know the steeplejacks visiting their village. And quite often the villagers would not have the steeplejacks in their homes, they were frightened of them.

****

From the minute the steeplejacks arrived, the people of the village probably knew it wouldn't be too long, before the vicar was tapping up the congregation for a few quid to cover the work. They got the job of repairing the steeple at Sharnbrook church, Bedfordshire, after it had been struck by lightning.

SHARNBROOK.

Messrs. J. T. Aliens and Sons, of Leicester, have commenced to repair the Church spire, which was recently struck by lightning. The placing of the ladders and the operations around the weather cock, are being watched with great interest.

SHARNBROOK

Messrs. J. T. Aliens and sons, of Leicester, have commenced to repair the church spire, which was recently struck by lightning. The placing of the ladders and the operations around the weathercock, are being watched with great interest.

****

Most of, it not all of the family have experienced people spelling our name wrong at some point. I think it annoys most of us a little bit. Atkines, akins, Aitkens, but this one in the article above is a new one on me. Aliens !!! An unusual mis-spelling, a typo probably. The same newspaper spelt it correctly in the follow up article after the work had been done.

Dundas had charge of the arrangements. Messrs. J. T. Akiens and Sons, of Leicester, have completed their repairs to the church spire. The operation of placing the weather-cock on top was watched by a good number of people on Tuesday evening. Harold Akiens, who is only 15 years of age, performed this duty at a height of 147 feet. New stone has been used round the steeple, making it practically a new one. A new spindle-core has been put in, and the "cock" has been re-gilded and given a new head and tail. It weighed just 22 lbs.

Messrs. J. T. Akiens and sons, of Leicester, have completed their repairs to the church spire. The operation of placing the weathercock on top was watched by a good number of people on Tuesday evening. Harold Akiens who is only 15 years of age, performed this duty at a height of 147 feet. New stone has been used round the steeple, making it practically a new one. A new spindle core has been put in. and the "cock" has been reguilded and given a new head and tail. It weighed just 22 lbs.

****

MARKET HARBOROUGH CHURCH SPIRE.

It has been found necessary to undertake extensive repairs to the spire of the Parish Church.

A thorough inspection has been made by Messrs. Stockdale Harrison and Sons, architects, Leicester, whose report shows that the summit of the spire is in a dangerous condition for some twelve or fifteen feet down, the stonework having bulged out and caused this length to be thrown out of the perpendicular. It will be therefore requisite that the whole be taken down and rebuilt.

Nearly all the crockets are defective, and are either loose or broken; these will require to be re-fixed in cement, and in some cases new ones will have to be supplied.

All the four top spirelight windows require new hoodstones, together with new stone to top of mullions. The lower spirelight windows require new apex stones with three new crosses.

The architects strongly advise that attention be given at once to the vane and crockets, as they are in a dangerous condition.

An estimate has been received from Messrs. J. T. Akires and Sons, who place the cost of repairs at £160, and they have been asked to proceed with the work without delay; this does not include the pointing of inside the spire, which on subsequent examination the Architect said was necessary to save heavy expenditure in the near future. The total cost, therefore, will be over £200.

It has been decided to place the £50 given to the vicar and churchwardens by the representatives of the late Mr. W. W. Wartnaby at the head of a list of subscriptions to the restoration fund, and the Churchwardens ask that generous contributions may be added by all who take an interest in the preservation of an ancient building which, if allowed to fall into decay, would be an irremediable loss to the town.

Contributions should be sent to the Churchwardens:—

MARKET HARBOROUGH CHURCH SPIRE

It has been found necessary to undertake extensive repairs to the spire of the Parish Church.

A thorough inspection has been made by Messrs. Stockdale Harrison and Sons, architects, Leicester, whose report shows that the summit of the spire is in a dangerous condition for some twelve or fifteen feet down, the stonework having bulged out and caused this length to be thrown out of the perpendicular.

It will be therefore requisite that the whole thing be taken down and rebuilt.

Nearly all the crockets are defective, and are either loose or broken ; these will require to be re-fixed in cement, and in some cases new ones will have to be supplied.

All four top spire light windows require new hood stones, together with new stone to top of mullions. The lower spire light windows require new apex stones with three new crosses.

The architects strongly advise that attention be given at once to the vane and crockets as they are in a dangerous condition. An estimate has been received from Messrs. J. T. Akiens and sons, who place the cost of repairs at £160, and they have been asked to proceed with the work without delay ; this does not include the pointing of inside the spire, which on subsequent examination the Architect said it was necessary to save heavy expenditure in the near future. The total cost therefore , will be over £200.

It has been decided to place the £50 given to the vicar and church wardens by the representative of the late Mr. W. W. Wartnaby at the head of a list of subscriptions to the restoration fund and the churchwardens ask that generous contributions may be added by all who take an interest in the preservation of an ancient building which, if allowed to fall into decay, would be an irremediable loss to the town.

Contributions should be sent to the church wardens.

****

The work they did on the Market Harborough church steeple was priced at £200. You could buy a brand new 4 bedroom semi detached house for that money at that time. So it was a considerable job to take on. They would take the whole top off the steeple stone by stone, and rebuild it down on the ground like this one in the picture above. So they knew exactly what they were doing, for when it came to rebuilding it high up on the top of the church.

Pictured in the next newspaper are a few of the family and some of the locals who watched them carry out the repairs. Great aunt Lydia performed the final part of the job placing the weathercock back on the top of the steeple.

RENOVATIONS to Market Harborough Church spire bring to mind similar operations in October, 1911, when Miss Lydia Akiens, a daughter of the head of the Leicester steeplejack firm, climbed to the top of the spire and replaced the weathercock "bright in its gold film and gaily decorated with ribbon." This picture is believed to have been taken just before the ascent, with, it is thought, the intrepid Miss Lydia in the centre of the group. Do any of our readers recognise any others on the picture?

Renovations to Market Harborough Church Spire bring to mind similar operations in October 1911,,when Miss Lydia Akiens, a daughter of the head of the steeplejack firm, climbed to the top of the spire and replaced the weathercock. " Bright in its Gold trim and gaily decorated with ribbon." This picture is believed to have been taken just before the ascent, with, it is thought, the intrepid Miss Lydia in the centre of the group.

****

The next article was written about the family after a lightning strike when they were working on the steeple.

....

NARROW ESCAPE ON STEEPLE

Lightning Strikes High Spire.

MEN UNTOUCHED. -

Violent Storms In London District.

VIOLENT storms swept over London and its environs' yesterday, several houses being struck by lightning and considerable damage done. Several people had narrow escapes from injury.

The Leicester firm of Steeplejacks the Akiens, were working on the church steeple in Canonbury, North London, had wonderful escapes from injury when the steeple was struck by lightning.

Smoke emerged from the steeple and the steeplejacks, together with onlookers down on the ground, thought the rope by which the men were suspended had caught fire.

****

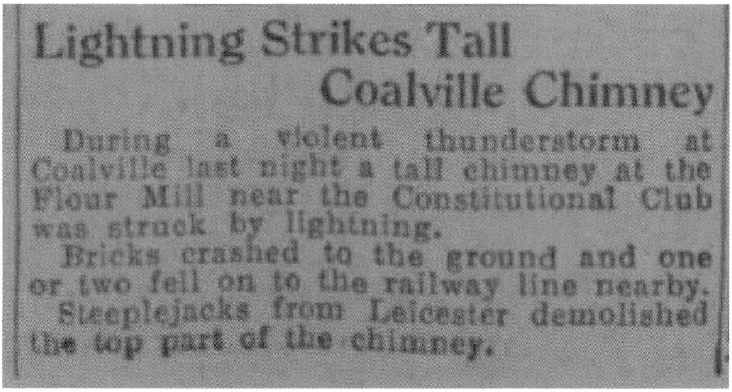

Lightning Strikes Tall Coalville Chimney

During a violent thunderstorm at Coalville last night a tall chimney at the Flour Mill near the Constitutional Club was struck by lightning.
Bricks crashed to the ground and one or two fell on to the railway line nearby. Steeplejacks from Leicester demolished the top part of the chimney.

Lightning Strikes Tall Coalville Chimney

During a violent thunderstorm at Coalville last night a tall chimney at the flour mill near the constitutional club was struck by lightning. Bricks crashed to the ground and one or two fell on to the railway line nearby. Steeplejacks from Leicester demolished the top part of the chimney.

****

40

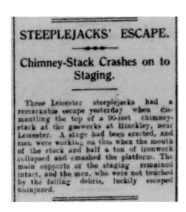

STEEPLEJACKS' ESCAPE.

Chimney-Stack Crashes on to Staging.

Three Leicester steeplejacks had a remarkable escape yesterday when dismantling the top of a 90-feet chimney-stack at the gasworks at Hinckley, near Leicester. A stage had been erected, and men were working on this when the mouth of the stack and half a ton of ironwork collapsed and smashed the platform. The main supports of the staging remained intact, and the men, who were not touched by the falling debris, luckily escaped uninjured.

STEEPLEJACKS ESCAPE

Chimney Stack Crashes on to staging.

Three Leicester steeplejacks had a remarkable escape yesterday when dismantling the top of a 90 feet chimney stack at the gas works at Hinkley, near Leicester. A stage had been erected, and men were working on this when the mouth of the stack and half a ton of ironwork collapsed and smashed the platform. The main supports of the staging remained intact, and the men who were not touch by the falling debris, luckily escaped uninjured.

****

A couple of instances where church spires were struck by lightning. It was lucky in these cases lives were not lost.

A CHURCH SPIRE DESTROYED BY LIGHTNING.— Early on Friday morning a terrible thunderstorm raged at Kidwelly, Carmarthenshire. The lightning struck the church spire, which was 180 feet high, and hurled 30 feet of it down, some of the stones being thrown to a distance of 300 yards. Stones fell through the roofs of adjoining houses, the inmates in bed having narrow escapes. A further portion of the spire is in a dangerous condition, and is being pulled down

A CHURCH SPIRE DESTROYED BY LIGHTNING.—

Early on Friday morning a terridble thunderstorm raged at Kidwelly, Carmarthenshire. The lightning struck the church spire, which was 180 feet high, and hurled 30 feet of it down, some of the stones being thrown a distance of 300 yards. Stomnes fell through roofs of adjoining houses, the inmates in bed having narrow escapes. A further portion of the spire is in a dangerous condition, and is being pulled down…

****

SPIRE COLLAPSES.

Steeple Struck by Lightning at Falkirk.

A 150 feet steeple at Falkirk occupying a commanding- position the High Street, struck by lightning yesterday afternoon. The top part of the spire collapsed and tons of masonry crashed on the thoroughfare and roofs of tenements. Several persons were injured and many had narrow escapes from death. A horse standing in the street was buried beneath the debris and killed.

****

There were thousands and thousands of chimneys in cities all over the country back then. They used to say that Lancashire had a forest of chimneys they had so many at one time. That's why the family bought property up there, so they had a base to work from. Only a tiny number of them are left today. There are over 20 in this one small area of Leicester pictured next. The family will have worked on some of these.

They made the steeples safe, so people could go and pray, during some very dark times in England's history. People today don't realise just how important

43

the steeplejacks work was. Why would they, most of it happened before most people alive today were born.

When a baby was born in the family, astonishingly, the father would carry the new born to the top of a chimney in one arm, to give the baby its first glimpse of the world he or she had been born into. Its hard to believe anyone would do that with a new born baby in this day and age, but apparently they did. A few people in the family have told me that story. I wasn`t sure whether to believe that one either, until i found this next article.

> A remarkable climbing record was established at Hinckley, when, notwithstanding rain, cold, and fog, three generations of a well-known family of Leicester steeplejacks, climbed the steeple of the parish church, 200 feet high. The baby's mother and grandmother anxiously witnessed the feat from the church tower. The younger carried the baby in one arm and climbed with the other, his performance being all the more remarkable owing to the ladders being coated with ice. At the top he placed the baby on the spot, usually occupied by the weather cock.

A remarkable climbing record was established at Hinkley, when, not with standing the rain, cold, and fog, three generations of a well known family of Leicester steeplejacks, climbed the parish church, 200 feet high. The baby`s mother and grandmother anxiously witnessed the feat from the church tower. The younger carried the baby in one arm and climbed with the other, his performance being all the more remarkable owing to the ladders being coated with ice. At the top placed the baby on the spot usually occupied by the weather cock.

****

Iv read some terrible accounts of things that happened to some of these men while researching how steeplejacks lives were in general in years gone by. But this next one made me laugh. A chimney fell in the wrong direction in Bolton, after a cock up by the steeplejack who dropped it. He had to compensate every person and business for the clean up of their clothes, shop fronts and windows.

People Plastered With Mud When Chimney is Felled.

Windows of shops and houses were smashed and more than 100 people covered from head to foot by mud which showered over a quarter of a mile area in Bolton, when the 250 foot chimney of the Derby Mill, High street was felled. Mud stones broken bottles and other debris were flung nearly 100 feet into the air and rained down on to houses and half a dozen neighbouring roads.

* * * * * * * * * * * * * * * * *

Mr. Akiens has split his skull, injured his ribs and received extensive bruises in falling from chimneys. He fell 50 feet from a chimney at the Swain-street Institution, Leicester, 75 feet from a chimney in Essex and 80 feet from a chimney at York. In each case he made a quick recovery, but,

The above article was written about one of the family, im not exactly sure who it was, I have an idea but hopefully someone in the family can tell me. He also fell a few times and survived.

45

AN American journalist recently gave a talk in the B.B.C. programmes on walking the high wire at a circus. He performed the feat himself for the sake of "copy." Which reminds me of an invitation extended to me by a Leicester steeplejack. He offered to take me up a 200ft. chimney at Aylestone electricity station.

"You'll be all right," he promised, but I wasn't having any.

My interviewee was Mr. Akiens, a member of a remarkable family.

The family was a big one—there were 16 children—and four daughters and eight sons became steeplejacks.

TWICE the family has claimed the distinction of world championship.

AN American journalist recently gave a talk in the B.B.C programmes on walking the high wire at a circus. He performed the feat himself for the sake of "copy." Which reminds me of an invitation extended to me by a Leicester steeplejack. He offered to take me up a 200 foot chimney at Aylestone electricity station. " You`ll be alright." He promised, but I wasn't having any of it.

My interviewee was Mr Akiens, a member of a remarkable family. The family was a big one- there were16 children-and four daughters and eight sons became steeplejacks. Twice the family have claimed the distinction of world. Championship.

****

There were dozens of steeplejacks across the different branches and generations of the family. There were 12 in granddads generation alone. All Five children in my dads generation went up chimneys. Many of the women in the family did as well.

46

The places that women get to nowadays

THE SORT OF JOB YOU CAN LOOK UP TO

The places that women get to nowadays

THE SORT OF JOB YOU CAN LOOK UP TO

WOMEN taxi-drivers, land girl, tram conductresses, the list of male occupations undertaken by women because of the war is a lengthy one, but there is surely no more unusual job for female hands, and nerve to tackle than that of steeplejack or steeplejill. The weather-cock on the steeple of St. Mark's Church, Leicester, was fixed there by a Leicester woman who was a world champion steeplejack.

Three of her sisters and her mother also worked in the trade. A quintette of female steeplejacks is as rare as quintuplets, but the Akiens family, of Leicester, are remarkable people. An artist could put Ripley out of business by illustrating their astonishing adventures and feats.

47

These former female steeplejacks do not care to talk of their experiences. It seems that though the public was literally obliged to look up to them to see them engaged at their work, the public also figuratively and frequently looked down on them for undertaking that work.

The mother of the four steeple-jills, the late Mrs. J. T. Akiens, often used to lend a hand when money for wages was scarce during the early days of the concern. Mrs. Akiens frequently assisted her husband during the last war, when he executed important Government contracts.

****

The work they did during both the wars was never reported in the newspapers at the time. My granddad told me of a few different jobs he did during world war two, painting radio towers twice as tall as any chimney he ever worked on was one of them. One of them was a tall story even by his standards. Another job he said did, was driving trucks for the army for 6 months for some reason. They must have needed a maniac, ive witnessed his driving first hand.

This article below is taken from the next feature written about them, telling of the dangerous work other steeplejacks wouldn`t take on. An example of the dirty work they did. The sort of work the family never turned down in all those years climbing.

the steeple-jacks, Messrs. J. T. Akiens and Sons, of Leicester practically built the stack himself. The centre of the erection was tested, on completion, by the architects, and found to be only half an inch out of plumb each way, which is considered exceedingly satisfactory. The work of demolition was started by another steeple-climber, but he found the work too risky, because the sulphur had eaten away the material, which was, consequently, very loose. A wire was immediately sent to Messrs. Akiens, one of the firm arrived the same night, and in four days the stack was taken down.

AT THE STACK HEAD.

INTERVIEWING A
"STEEPLE-JACK" AT EXETER.

NOVEL EXPERIENCE.

(SPECIAL TO THE "GAZETTE.")

About two months ago the work of demolishing a large chimney stack at the brick
yard of Messrs. J. Hancock and Son, Clifton
Hill, Exeter, was started. To-day a new chim-

This next article was a large feature printed in 1908. Some of these articles go into detail some of the dangers they faced daily, from the wind, rotting brickwork and toxic fumes pouring out of chimneys and overcoming people. Many steeplejacks lost their lives to all of these dangers.

AT THE STACK HEAD :

INTERVIEWING A STEEPLE-JACK AT EXETER.

NOVEL EXPERIENCE. (SPECIAL TO THE GAZETTE)

About two months ago the work of demolishing a large chimney stack at the brick yard of Messrs. J. Hancock and son, Clifton Hill, Exeter, was started. Today a new chimney of more formidable dimensions stands in its place. The task of transition has been somewhat hazzardous, but carried through without mishap.

The old chimney was a circular stack, about 125 feet in height, measured from the ground. The new one, which has been constructed from the ground line, is a solid brick octagonal chimney, with a 2ft 7 1/2 inch thick wall at the base, and a 9 inch wall at the top. The outside diameter at the base is 15 feet, and at the summit 6 feet : the inside diameters are 8 feet and 4 ft 6 respectively. The height is the same as that of the old stack. There are two moulded bands, and a moulded brick cap : all the moulded work and the 800,000 bricks used were supplied by Messrs. J. Hancock and son:, of Topsham road, Exeter : The architects, Messrs. J. M. and Allan J Pinn, of Bedford Circus:

The Steeplejacks, Messrs J. T. Akiens and Sons of Leicester, practically built the stack himself. The centre of the erection was tested on completion by architects, and was found to be only half an inch out of plumb each way, which is considered to be exceedingly satisfactory.

The work of demolition was started by another steeple climber, but he found the work too risky, because the sulphur had eaten away the material, which was, consequently, very loose. A wire was immediately sent to Messrs Akiens, one of the firm arrived the same night, and in Four days the stack was taken down.

One of our representatives who went to the works in Clifton Hill to find out a few particulars was immediately offered the opportunity of ascending the chimney by Mr. Anderson who is connected with the firm. The acceptance of the offer, to be candid, was more tardily given than the offering, but still, given, and after a blank refusal to be hoisted up the outside by the nerveless steeplejack, the ascent began from the inside.

The first part of the journey was practically in darkness, because there was a platform across the top, and consequently, no inlet for light until that was lifted. Strapped to the seat, in form like a swing, with the "jack" standing on it behind to steer a straight course, and with pious wishes from those below solemnly received, the two daring adventurers were brought to the summit by means of a pulley. The sensation was very similar to that experienced in the London tube railway lifts- a dreamy idea of motion, which, if allowed to have its natural effect leaves a semi conscious feeling that the motion is both ways, or that it is in no obvious or perceptible direction.

When the platform at the top was raised a flood of light entered, and the possibility of a drop became more conceivable than in the darkness. Once at the top, the strap was removed, and a wary peep was hazarded over the edge, though the inclination to hold back was strong. A splendid view of the city and the surroundings was was the reward. Nothing was more prominent than the fine old sanctuary of the diocese, standing out with dignity in the foreground. Over the hills behind it the Crimson of the sunset sky, that brilliant Crimson of

50

misty nights- gave the old city a serene and, as it seemed, an appropriate setting.

The Haldon hills and the estuary of the river Exe could also be distinguished, but the Dartmoor summits were obscured by the fog. At the same time, there was nothing exceptional in the prospect, unless it be gazing down upon the tops of the immediate houses, for similar sights of scenery can be seen, of course from the hill tops.

Meanwhile the "Jack" had been explaining various technicalities of his work, and left a rather hazy impression on ones mind, but soon the contempt bred by familiarity had risen to such a stage that the notebook and pencil were slowly withdrawn from the pockets, and the "jack" was telling how it was possible- contrary to what has been contended by some- to look down "dead" straight as it were and how with glasses he could distinguish what coin any man might hold in his hand below. Of course, he went on to explain, he had to lean out over the edge- and he did so, balancing himself by one leg from the knee downwards. An involuntary hint that perhaps it was time to descend had the necessary effect, and the interview continued.

John Thomas Akiens junior, comes of a climbing stock, and he says that his family, the members of which have been doing similar work for 200 years, are the oldest climbing family in England. He himself started when he was about 4 years old, but his young sister Lydia, when under 12 months of age, climbed 20 feet. This year, Akiens has beaten the world climbing record.

His mother has also done a considerable amount of climbing, and his father, has had many thrilling experiences and many close encounters with death, working on such dangerous chimneys and steeples.

Akiens has been a teetotaller all his life, and every man on his firm in Burton is forbidden to take alcohol; they are not even allowed to enter licensed premises to purchase tobacco or cigarettes, on pain of instant dismissal, for the absolute necessity of a level head and a steady eye is patent to all.

The stacks are climbed in the first instance externally by means of ladders and spikes. A ladder about 16 feet in length is run up and the jack knocks in a spike as far up as he can reach, and lashes another ladder to it, that continues until ladder by ladder the top is reached, and there`s one continuous means of ascent. Akiens had to come away in such a hurry that he was unable to bring the usual appliances so he had to use the ordinary cumbrous building ladders.

The builder said that Akiens stood on top on the top of the stack, and worked away with a pick as fearlessly as if he were on terra firma, and as a matter of fact, on the return from this unusual journey to the chimney stack summit, Akiens said he should like to know the sensation experienced by people unaccustomed to such heights. He had started so early that he had forgotten he ever had to make a start but, of course, ascending on the inside gave a gave a considerably greater feeling of security than on the outside. The descent down the dark way was soon accomplished and our representative left, feeling a man of more parts than before, and a man of some daring.

****

BABY STEEPLEJACKS :

110 FT CHIMNEY CLIMBED BY A BOY OF FIVE

1907 : At St. Helens yesterday, three of the younger members of the family of Mr. Akiens, the well known Leicester steeplejack, ascended one of the chimneys at the Roughdale brick and tile works.

Mr. Akiens has been anxious for some time to match his daughter Lydia aged 15, against any other lady climber in the world. She has made several journeys to the top of chimneys over 150ft high, and yesterday the girl mounted to the platform from which one of the Roughdale chimneys is being repaired, 110ft from the ground, in 1 min 5 seconds. She was followed by her brother Baden Akiens aged five years old, who as an extra test, was allowed to climb the ladders in his clogs. Two years ago when he had just turned three, he climbed to the top of the 150ft chimney at Roughdales. Yesterday he was soon on top, waving his hand to those below. After Baden came Gertrude, aged six, who also went up the ladders and remained there for some time on the scaffolding at the top. Tom Akiens aged 18, is amazingly nimble on the ladders, and he yesterday descended over 150 feet in 15 seconds. They are all trained from infancy, and yesterday the baby, William Akiens aged just over a year, struggled up several rungs of the ladder in an endeavour to catch his brother.

****

Great uncle Tom Akiens descended over 150 feet in 15 seconds, over ten feet every second. You couldn't fall from a chimney much faster than that. And he was still a kid at the time. That was one of the world records he held. They were in court several times for this offence, allowing the kids to climb dangerous chimneys for public exhibitions. The Home Secretary got involved as this next newspaper reported on the same case.

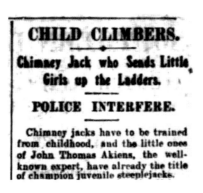

CHILD CLIMBERS.

Chimney Jack who Sends Little Girls up the Ladders.

POLICE INTERFERE.

Chimney jacks have to be trained from childhood, and the little ones of John Thomas Akiens, the well-known expert, have already the title of champion juvenile steeplejacks.

They were up court a few times for the offences of endangering the children. Granddad never got caught for it tho when he took my dad, his brother and sisters up chimneys.

Great Aunt Lydia climbed over 20 feet before she was even a year old. Hard to believe, but probably easier to believe when you consider the family already had over 200 years experience climbing by this time. In this newspaper article below, one of my great uncles climbed a 150 foot chimney when he was just Three years old ! Two years later he did it in his clogs as an extra test ! Who in their right minds would let their 3 year old do that in this day and age, absolute madness, but they did.

JUVENILE STEEPLEJACKS

WONDERFUL PERFORMANCES

Parent in the Police Court.

At St. Helens, today, John Thomas Akiens, the well known Leicester steeplejack, who has been employed for some time in the St. Helens district, was summoned on four information`s for causing his children to ascend a chimney at the Roughdale Brick Works, and thereby exposing them to danger.

54

There were two summonses in respect of a boy, Baden Akiens, aged five, one charge in respect of Gertrude, aged seven and the fourth in respect of a girl aged 15, named Lydia.
Defendant said he must admit that the children climbed the chimney, but said it was not as a public exhibition.

The chief constable said the proceedings arose out of a challenge issued by the defendant to establish who was the youngest and most nimble steeplejack in the world. In the Liverpool Weekly post on August 24th, a paragraph appeared which stated that miss Lydia Akiens, the fifteen year old Leicester girl, is declared to be not only the youngest but the Champion female steeplejack of the world.

A challenge was recently issued on her behalf for a chimney or church climbing competition, but no one has been found to take up the challenge. It was then announced that the girl was about to climb a chimney 400ft. high at Liverpool, and that the event was to be recorded by cinematograph. Later a long report appeared in the Liverpool Daily Post and Mercury to the effect that Akiens had allowed three of his children to climb a chimney 110 ft. high.

Roughdales Brick works

The report stated that the question of who is the youngest steeplejack in the Kingdom was probably settled for some time to come yesterday in St. Helens,

55

when three of the younger members of the family of Mr Akiens the well known Leicester Steeplejack, ascended one of the chimneys of the Roughdale Brick and Tile Works. In this report it was stated that the Akiens family were all trained from infancy, and that Mr Akiens claims that Gertrude and Baden are the youngest chimneys climbers in the world, and that his daughter Lydia will beat any other lady climber.

COMMUNICATIONS FROM THE HOME SECRETARY

He had received communications from the home secretary on the matter, and he found that the climbs took place. It was true that the public were not admitted to the works, but there was quite a number of people outside who witnessed the performance, and there could be no doubt, that it was a public exhibition and highly dangerous, and he asked the bench to impose such a penalty as would deter anyone else from doing this kind of thing.

The Chairman (Mr F. Dromgoole) : was this performance used for cinematograph purposes ?
The chief Constable : No. The cinematograph people never turned up.
The clerk read the section of the dangerous Performances of Children act 1897, under which females under 18 and males under 16 were debarred from taking part in a dangerous performance.

CLIMB UNATTENDED.

Mr T. Stephene, manager of the Roughdale Brick and Tile Works, said that one of their chimneys was at present under repair. Defendant had the contract. On Tuesday, the 10th, he saw the children go up the chimney. The two younger children were closely followed by the defendants son. This was done without his permission.

The girl Lydia climbed the chimney unattended. He considered it dangerous for the younger children, and he posted a notice at the base of the chimney prohibiting any of the workmen from going up. He did this because he was responsible for the workmen. On Wednesday, the 11th, he was present when Detective Roe came to the works, and Baden the boy of five, went up in his presence. The following day he told the defendant that he must not take children up again.

The Chairman : Did you know the children were going up ? You had heard about it ? - "Yes "
And you didn`t attempt to prevent them ? "No, because he told me he was taking the whole responsibility."
They were not secured in any way ? They might have slipped from the ladder. - "I should say they were secured by their brother behind them"
But they were not tied to the ladder ? - "No"
And they might have fallen if their feet had slipped ? -"They scarcely could, because their brother had them before him"
By defendant : Did they go up two together ? -"No"
Only one at a time ? -"Yes"
And did my son go up with each one? -"Yes"
The Chairman : Do you mean that he was so close to them that he could have caught them if they had slipped ? -"Yes ; the girl went up by herself, but the two younger ones were followed up by the brother."
The Chief Constable : They all went up unattended ? Witness -"No"
William Piercey, kiln setter, Walkers lane, described the way in which the children went up. The brother was close behind them, and could catch them if anything went wrong. There were a large number of people watching in the lane"

Detective Roe said he went to Roughdales on the 11th, and asked the defendant if he could supply him with particulars of the climb that had taken place the previous day. They discussed the reports in the papers, and whilst he was there the boy Baden went up the chimney, followed by the defendant.

The Chairman : You didn`t attempt to prevent that ? -"No, i did not disclose my identity"
The Chief Constable : He thought you were a press representative ? - "Yes : he asked me what paper my report was for, and i said i didn`t exactly represent any particular paper, but no doubt a report of the affair would appear in the papers"

The defendant, in a long statement, said it had been custom in his family to train the children from the moment they could walk.

For over 200 hundred years they trained the children right from infancy to climb, and all through he had never been told that they were doing anything wrong.

The Chairman asked if defendant proposed to make the girl Lydia who claimed to be the champion lady climber, a chimney Jack.

Defendant said he trained all his children to climb, as well as to swim, so that they would be able to escape from fire or water. He never made a public exhibition, but the child frequently got on the ladder.

The clerk : What age were you when you first got on the ladder ?

Defendant : "I can hardly tell you. I was very small. I was bought up to it as soon as i could walk"

The Chairman asked if the defendant had made arrangements for a display of this kind. Defendant said there was a statement in some of the papers that said his daughter would climb a chimney stack in Liverpool 400 feet in height, but he did not know anything about it.

John Thomas Akiens, the son, aged twenty, described how he ascended the chimney in company with his younger sister and brother. They never went alone. It was impossible for them to fall. They had a strap around their waist, on which a hook, which could be attached to the ladder, and by which they could rest.

The magistrates considered the case in private, and the Chairman announced that they considered it to be objectionable and dangerous.

The defendant must not let it occur again, but, seeing that he had entered upon it under a misunderstanding, they would bind him over in his own surety of £5 and two sureties of £2 10s each, not allow this to occur again, and he must pay the costs of these sureties. Akiens asked what age an apprentice must be before he could allow him to ascend the chimney.

The Clerk : Eighteen in the case of a girl and sixteen in the case of a boy.

****

The defendant, in a long statement, said it had been a custom in
his family to train the children from
the moment they could walk.

58

The defendant made a long statement to the court, i bet he did. They would argue til they were blue in the face, if they were anything like granddad was. Quite a few times dad was in the pub with granddad, and he`d be arguing a point with someone. The bloke knew granddad was wrong, dad knew granddad was wrong, even granddad himself knew he was wrong, but he would not back down or give in to the bloke. He would stick him out that he was right. It used to make dad laugh.

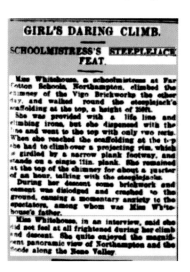

'Twas Miss Whitehurst, ma'am. The Vigo brickyard chimney she climbed with steeplejack J. Akiens in September, 1913, wasn't the world's second tallest.
But it was the fourth tallest in England, a nerve-shattering 250ft, and the top platform she walked round was only 11 inches wide!

The kids would race against each other on opposite sides of the chimneys up ladders for exhibitions, to help raise their public profile possibly, and maybe raise a few quid for good causes while they were at it. It drew in the crowds and helped promote the work they did. The newspaper above was one example of how great granddad went about getting the families name known. The article below is the same story in greater detail.

GIRL'S DARING CLIMB.

SCHOOLMISTRESS'S STEEPLEJACK FEAT.

Miss Whitehouse, a schoolmistress at Far Cotton Schools, Northampton, climbed the chimney of the Vigo Brickworks the other day, and walked round the steeplejack's scaffolding at the top, a height of 250ft.
She was provided with a life line and climbing irons, but she dispensed with the line and went to the top with only two rests. When she reached the scaffolding at the top she had to climb over a projecting rim, which is girdled by a narrow plank footway, and stands on a single 11in. plank. She remained at the top of the chimney for about a quarter of an hour, talking with the steeplejacks.
During her descent some brickwork and cement was dislodged and crashed to the ground, causing a momentary anxiety to the spectators, among whom was Miss Whitehouse's father.
Miss Whitehouse, in an interview, said she did not feel at all frightened during her climb and descent. She quite enjoyed the magnificent panoramic view of Northampton and the woods along the Nene Valley.

GIRL`S DARING CLIMB

SCHOOL MISTRESS`S STEEPLEJACK FEAT

Miss Whitehouse, a school mistress at Far Cotton school, Northampton, climbed the Vigo brickworks the other day, and walked round the steeplejacks scaffolding at the top, a height of 250 feet.

She was provided with a lifeline and climbing irons, but she dispensed with the line and went to the top with only two rests. When she reached the top she had to climb over a projecting rim, which is girdled by a narrow plank footway, and stands on a simple 11 inch plank. She remained at the top of the chimney for about a quarter of an hour, talking with the steeplejacks.

During her descent some brickwork and cement was dislodged and crashed to the ground, causing a momentary anxiety to the spectators, among whom was miss Whitehouses father.

Miss Whitehouse, in an interview, said she did not feel at all frightened during her climb and descent. She quite enjoyed the magnificent panoramic view of Northampton and the floods along the Nene valley.

＊＊＊＊＊＊＊＊＊＊＊＊＊＊＊＊＊

> The Leicester steeple-jack was once on the top of the Church steeple at Bedford, when one of his mates came up drunk, and wanted to fight him. " We were standing (he says) on two planks about 24 inches wide, and it gave me a turn, you can think. But I gripped him by the throat, and when I had done with him there wasn't an ounce of fight left in him. I tied him up to the cage and left him there until he'd slept a bit of it off.
>
> The same man tells how one of his workmen once saved himself from instant death by a plucky

I heard all sorts of stories from the family and people that knew them, about some of the work they did and some of the things they got up to. I never knew whether to believe them or not, they just seemed too far fetched. Until i found many of them online in lots of newspapers from that time.

Many of them have turned out to be true. One story i havent found any proof of yet, is that before the family were steeeplejacks there was a hangman in the family somewhere, an executioner. Maybe that will turn out to be true, maybe it won`t. A Canadian relative recently got in touch after finding this books website, we share the same grt grt, grt, grand parents. She told me some of the family moved to the U.S and started up a business, in death valley.

Below :   A drunken work mate wanted a fight with grt grt granddad in 1895, at the top of a church steeple in Bedford, so he throttled him a bit, tied him to the cage, and let him sleep it off. The same article was published in another newspaper below and also tells of how the chimneys rocked and swayed in the high winds.

THE ROCKING OF THE SHAFT.

There is an interesting description of the building of the ladders length by length up the face of the shaft. " I never get to the last ladder without a bit of a quake, " Said the steeplejack : - " What does it feel like up there ? Is a chimney worse to stand upon than a steeple ?" "There`s no comparing them. For one thing, your ledge on which you stand is not much more than 1ft. wide, and you`ve a drop on both sides of you. There`s a good deal of heat, likely enough coming from the flue of the shaft, and, added to that, the whole chimney rocks and sways whenever the wind is high in a way that would turn you sick. Ive known a tall shaft to swing nearly a foot either way in a gale. That doesn`t sound much; but you stand up there while the game is going on, and i`ll bet my life you say your prayers if you never said them before. Run up with me now and try it ?"

AN INVITATION TO FIGHT

The invitation to run up and try it for himself was not accepted by the writer. So the Steeplejack told of an invitation he had himself accepted on the top of a steeple at Bedford-. " A mate of mine came up drunk and wanted to fight me. We were standing on two planks about 24" wide, and it gave me a turn, you can think. But I gripped him by the throat, and when I was done with him there wasn`t an ounce of fight left in him" "How did he get down again?" "Oh that was easy enough. I tied him to the cage and left him there until he slept a bit of it off"

****

In 1912 seven years before this next article was written, a steeplejack fell to his death on the pavement from St Alkmunds, in front of a large crowd of people. There had been deaths on many of the chimneys and steeples they worked on.

STEEPLE-JACKS ON ST. ALKMUNDS :

62

REPAIRS THAT WERE URGENTLY CALLED FOR.

St. Alkmunds

Derby experienced two distinct thrills last week. One came through the flying exploits of of Mr. Alan Cobham from a field at Sunny Hill - the other from the steeplejacks engaged on repair of St. Alkmunds Spire.

There is some appropriateness in the conjunction of these men, for each represented a high type of twentieth century nerve and intrepidity. There was clearly a bond of sympathy between them too, for one evening when the steeplejacks had made their hold on the spire secure as far as the weather cock itself. Mr. Alan Cobham beat up from the south and showed his appreciation of the rival artists` coolness and daring by making the circuit of St. Alkmunds at a closer range than he ever ventured on before or afterwards. The average airman, has no great liking for the work of the steeplejack. He regards it- tell it not in gath- as too dangerous! Many an airman we believe, has been challenged to ascend an exalted spire or mill chimney by means of a rope ladder, but we have never yet heard that the amiable exchange of pleasantries between professors of the two callings has led to business.

The present, of course is not the first occasion on which St. Alkmunds spire has been in need of the attentions of a steeplejack. On February 28th 1860, the town of Derby was swept by a great gale, which carried off about 10 feet of the spire, bring down with it the weather vane and ball, which fell through the roof of the church and did considerable damage to the pews, the old organ and the floor of the church. It was fortunate in many respects that the fall took place on the roof of the church at a period of the night when it was certain to be unoccupied.

Had the crashing masonry and vane descended on one of the houses round about bridge gate or St. Alkmunds churchyard there must almost inevitably have been loss of life- perhaps even on a serious scale.

That was during the long vicariate of Prebendary Abbey. Whilst the Rev. J. Stanley Owen was vicar the spire again demanded attention, but during the quarter of a century or so that has since elapsed there has been no further need of repairs until a few weeks ago, when it became evident that something had to be done, and quickly, to avert more serious trouble.

The services of Messrs. J. T. Akiens and sons, of Leicester, were called in, and

the report which they submitted on the state of the spire was of a serious character. Without going into technical details, it may be said that internally a good deal of mortar in the joints of the stone work is badly perished, while externally the top 12 feet of spire work is lifting dangerously, and a good deal of work is required to renew its former stability. The inside of the spire indeed, is in a very dilapidated condition, and altogether a good deal of attention is called for from the repairers.

The Akiens family, have been entrusted with this delicate and dangerous commission, are a family of steeplejacks. They train for their calling almost from the cradle. The whole family "go up" as they say. A daughter ascended St. Marks Leicester, and the church at Market Harborough to restore vanes.

The son who is engaged on St. Alkmunds has probably had the most thrilling escape from death that can be claimed by any man in the world. This was in November 1910, when he was fixing a lightening conductor on a chimney at Mrs. Wrights brick works at Sileby. A stiff wind was blowing at the time, and he had failed to clean all the clay off his boots, with the result that when the rain came his footing became insecure, and the wind did the rest.

A fall of 80 feet to the ground followed, but marvellous to relate, he escaped practically without injury. No man could have such a fall a second time without encountering certain death, or at the very least, terrible injuries that would make him a hopeless sample of humanity for the rest of his days. More terrible perhaps, because extending over over a period which seemed an age, was the experience he had at Thurmaston whilst repairing the widest chimney in Leicestershire.

The top of the chimney was very badly cracked, and whilst working at a height of 150 feet, the party, which numbered five, became conscious that ten tons of masonry had shifted, and threatened to topple over at any moment, bringing death and disaster to them all.

The only way of saving their lives was to make the brickwork secure, and to do this was a task of extraordinary peril that the barest movement of the workers threatened to bring down the whole of the masonry around them. It was a situation that called for all their nerve, but by stealth and skill it was eventually overcome, after the most racking four hours any of them had ever endured.

The perils of a steeplejacks calling are sufficiently obvious, and the risk of fall as from decaying and treacherous chimney tops is not the only foe they have to face. Take for instance the case of the man who was overcome by fumes whilst working on a big chimney in Sheffield last Saturday.

Cases of this kind are not in frequently encountered, and as far as it is possible to take precautionary measures they are taken beforehand. But the man in the street who looks at a chimney that has been found to stand in need of repair, can form no conception of the fearful state in which, on examination such structures are commonly found.

By their daring our steeplejacks make discoveries that are of the most vital importance to the people in the immediate neighbourhood and indicate repairs that should be dealt with at once. If men were not found willing to take these risks a great chimney might go from bad to worse, until at length a hurricane of unusual force would either send it over altogether, or displace such a mass of masonry as would create fearful havoc both to human life and surrounding property.

To that extent, therefore, the Steeplejack performs a service to mankind which we are perhaps a little too prone to overlook. Neither residents or passers by would care to run the risk of St. Alkmunds vane coming down with an unexpected crash as it did nearly 60 years ago.

****

> An encounter on Bottesford church tower with a lunatic, the ascent of Queniborough church tower to a height of 210 feet without the aid of ropes or ladders, the feat of hanging upside down at the top of a chimney at Frog Island . . . these are further random selections from the hefty repertoire of the Akiens family, and veracity enhances the thrill of each of their stories.

A few more snippets of tales in the previous article, written about the family in another newspaper. Notably, how one of them climbed over 200 feet to the top of Queniborough church steeple, without any ladders. Im not so sure it would be 210 feet, a lot of the heights of things were exaggerated in the papers. Still an impressive free climb though.

66

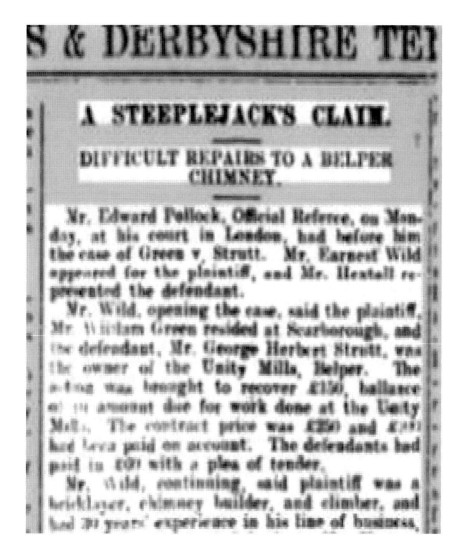

A STEEPLEJACK'S CLAIM.

DIFFICULT REPAIRS TO A BELPER CHIMNEY.

Mr. Edward Pollock, Official Referee, on Monday, at his court in London, had before him the case of Green v. Strutt. Mr. Earnest Wild appeared for the plaintiff, and Mr. Hextall represented the defendant.

Mr. Wild, opening the case, said the plaintiff, Mr. William Green resided at Scarborough, and the defendant, Mr. George Herbert Strutt, was the owner of the Unity Mills, Belper. The action was brought to recover £150, balance of the amount due for work done at the Unity Mills. The contract price was £250 and £100 had been paid on account. The defendants had paid in £50 with a plea of tender.

Mr. Wild, continuing, said plaintiff was a bricklayer, chimney builder, and climber, and had 30 years' experience in his line of business,

In this court case above Great granddad seemed to enjoy himself and gave the court a few laughs. He wasn`t bothered, he wasn`t in the dock this time, he was a witness for the prosecution. A wealthy mill owner was trying to rip off one of his rival steeplejack mates for a dangerous job he did. He took the opportunity to emphasise he was a better steeplejack than his mate was. The wealthy mill owner was a "Gentleman, and Chairman of the county council". No prizes for guessing who won that case.

A STEEPLEJACKS CLAIM

DIFFICULT REPAIRS TO A BELPER CHIMNEY

Mr. Edward Pollock, Official Referee, on Monday, at his court in London, had before him the case of Green V Strutt. Mr Earnest Wild appeared for the plaintiff and Mr Hextall represented the defendant.
Mr Wild, opening the case, said it was the plaintiff, Mr William Green resided at Scarborough, and the defendant, Mr George Herbert Strutt, was the owner of the unity mills, Belper. The action was brought to recover £150, balance of an amount due for work done at the unity mills. The contract price was £250 and £100 had been paid on account. The defendants had paid £100 with a plea of tender.

Mr Wild, continuing, said plaintiff was a brick layer, chimney builder, and climber, and had 30 years experience in his line of business. In 1905 the agent of defendant, Mr Hunter, Thought the chimney needed pointing and plaintiff was required to do the work. On the 28th July he entered on his task. Plaintiff when he got to the top of the chimney, discovered an Iron cap weighing seven tonnes, resting on brickwork nine inches thick. The cap was loose, and plaintiff was instructed to take it off, take down the chimney for nineteen feet from the top, point the chimney from top to the bottom, and make a good job of it. This work was carried out with considerable difficulty and danger.

The work was concluded on October 3rd, thus taking nine weeks and four days, and on sending his bill, including £100 for risk to himself, the defendant disputed the charge of £250, although plaintiff had said during the time he was engaged it would be that amount.

The plaintiff gave evidence in support of his case, and said no insurance company would insure his men when they knew the character of their work. His charges were fair and reasonable, and he would not tackle another job like it for £500, let alone £250.

The Official Referee : Were it possible the government might like to insure themselves. (Laughter)
I do not deny your work is dangerous. I do not mean it offensively, but as i understand it, you put a value on your life of £100 ? - "Yes, i have a wife and

family". Albert Green, son of the plaintiff, gave evidence as to the condition if the chimney and the work done.

The court adjourned and was resumed on Tuesday.

Mr John Thomas Akiens, builder and steeple climber, who had inspected the chimney, said the charges were reasonable.

Take the country through, there is no competition for work, is there not ? - "Yes, there is a lot of competition amongst us, i`m sorry to say" (laughter) Witness added that £150 would be a small amount for the work plaintiff did.

This chimney at Belper is 175 feet high, would be a commonplace height from your point of view ? - " I never take notice of the height, the height is play to me" (Laughter)

Given the right tackle when you are up it does not matter whether the chimney is 150 feet or 200 feet high ? -" It would not matter if the chimney were a thousand feet high if we had proper tackle to work with."

In these circumstances anyone can do the work ? - "Well, i do not know. It is nothing to me. I do not feel frightened. But those who are not used to the work and who go up tell me it is like looking down on a whole new world." (Laughter)

Mr Scott, (counsel for the plaintiff) in re-examination : How much would you have charged for this job? - "well, i don`t know"

The official Referee : There is competition, you know. (Laughter) Witness and plaintiff are rivals in trade, and Mr Akiens may wish to get a job from him.

Witness : Well i have been competing with him as far as that goes. Therefore it is hardly fair to ask me that question. Mr Green knows that in getting up in the air he has not a a shadow of a chance in getting up with me, it is a matter of quickness. (Laughter)

THE CASE FOR THE DEFENDANT

Mr. Hextall, addressing the court for the defendant, submitted that the £160 which Mr. Strutt was willing to pay was adequate for all that had been done. Mr. Strutt was a gentleman with very large possessions in Belper and other parts of Derbyshire. He was Chairman of the county council, and the last man in the world to endeavour to take advantage of a person in a position of the plaintiff. But he was advised that the sum he was ready to pay was sufficient to amply compensate plaintiff for the work done, and that the charge of £250 was out of all proportion to any demand which could be properly made. To claim £100 for risk and only £150 for the work done was an extraordinary position. He should call witnesses to prove that the £160 which Mr Strutt had offered to pay was quite sufficient to meet the value of the work executed, and evidence would be given that insurances of persons engaged in this class of work could be effected and were constantly entered into.

Mr John Hunt, of Belper, a magistrate for Derbyshire and manager for Mr. Strutt, said that he gave plaintiff the order to point the chimney. Later on the plaintiff drew his attention to the fact that the mortar of the brickwork was decaying under the cap. He said in his opinion it ought to come down.

He added that he knew it would be an awkward job to get the cap off, but he must charge as reasonably as he could.

Subsequently he ordered the chimney to be raised. All the materials used in the work were provided and paid for by Mr. Strutt, and he paid for all the labour on the ground. When plaintiff told him he thought his bill would be £250 he objected, and said it was very much more than he had dreamed of. When the bill was delivered he was advised that the charges were excessive, and he offered to pay £260 for the work. After evidence as to the tender of £60 had been given by the defendant, the referee intimated that he wished to hear no further evidence on behalf of defendant, and in giving judgement, said that the £160 which had been paid would repay the plaintiff handsomely for the work he had done, and that judgement be entered for the defendant, with costs subsequent to the payment into court of £60.

****

Another article that mentions Lydia, this time climbing a 400 foot chimney in Liverpool, wearing a bioscope, whatever that is. Below that there is the account of John Goldie, a well known Scotch steeplejack who fell from the tallest chimney in the country. A 480 foot chimney the family worked on a few years afterwards. Eight steeplejacks were killed working on it years later.

GIRL STEEPLEJACK.—Miss Lydie Akiens, the fifteen-year-old Leicester girl "steeplejack," will, it is stated, shortly climb a four hundred feet chimney shaft at Liverpool, when a bioscope apparatus will record her movements.

STEEPLEJACK'S TERRIBLE FALL.—The well-known Scotch steeplejack, John Goldie, met with a shocking death on Tuesday, while working on a chimney in Glasgow. The unfortunate man was on the top of the chimney when he was suddenly seen to reel and fall over the edge. The shaft is 488 feet high, and Goldie's body was literally smashed to a pulp.

STEEPLEJACKS TERRIBLE FALL - John Goldie

The well known Scotch steeplejack John Goldie, met with a shocking death on Tuesday, while working on a chimney in Glasgow. The unfortunate man was on the top of the chimney when he was suddenly seen to reel and fall over the edge. The shaft is 488 feet high, and Goldies body was literally smashed to a pulp.

****

Lydia Akiens, a 15 year old Leicester girl, is the champion girl steeplejack of the world, and does what the very thought of would cause thousands of men to shudder. She recently climbed and walked round the top of a 400 feet chimney.

This above article was written after she'd made the world record breaking climb. Another of the several records they held in the steeplejacking world.

Lydia Akiens, a 15 year old Leicester girl, is the champion girl steeplejack of the world and does what the very thought of would cause thousands of men to shudder, She recently climbed a 400 feet chimney

****

71

Mr Akiens worked on the tallest chimney in the country at Glasgow. Messrs. Akiens contracted to shorten the chimney 480 feet high, which had become unsafe. They later reduced it to 340 feet. Later when another firm were engaged in operations on the chimney, the stack collapsed and eight of the nine men working on it were killed, the ninth falling into a tank of water.

****

Great aunt Lydia and great aunt Rose, having their photos taken at a studio on Abbey park road.

They were very close sisters until well into their old age. They would almost run across the road, hardly looking to see if there was any traffic coming, to stop my Mam, when they were out shopping around Belgrave, to have a look in my pram. I was too young to actually remember them. They looked very different dolled up in these photos to what they wore at work.

72

Jesse Akiens, the boy-steeple-
jack, killed in a fall at
Leicester, and his sister standing on an unprotected staging.

BOY STEEPLEJACK

Jesse Akiens , the boy steeplejack killed in a fall at Leicester, and his sister standing on an unprotected staging.

****

THE CHAMPION LADY STEEPLEJACK. — In order to obtain unique photographs for a sale in connection with a church, Miss Lydia Akiens, aged nineteen years, the daughter of J. T. Akiens, a well-known steeplejack, of Leicester and St. Helens, climbed a steeple-jack's ladder to the top of the lofty spire of St. Mark's Church, 200 feet high. Having reached the top, Miss Akiens, camera in hand, coolly walked round the narrow, unprotected staging and snapshotted some fine views. So thrilling was the feat that many of the crowd below walked away, declaring they could watch her no longer. Miss Akiens claims to be the champion lady steeplejack of the world.

THE CHAMPION LADY STEEPLEJACK.

73

In order to obtain unique photographs for a sale in connection with a church, Miss Lydia Akiens (aged nineteen years, the daughter of J. T. Akiens, a well

known steeplejack, of Leicester and St Helens climbed a steeplejacks ladder to the top of the lofty spire of St Marks Church, 200ft high. Having reached the top, Miss Akiens, camera in hand, cooly walked round the narrow, unprotected staging, and snapshotted some fine views. So thrilling was the feat that many of the crowd below walked away, declaring they could watch her no longer. Miss Akiens is the champion lady steeplejack of the world.

Pictured below, Jesse inset and Lydia at the top of St Marks church, Leicester.

CLIMBING SISTERS.

THEY'RE BRITAIN'S ONLY "STEEPLEJILLS"!

From "The People's" Correspondent.

The claim to be Britain's only "steeple-jills" is made by two pretty Midland sisters aged nineteen and seventeen—

These "steeplejills" were truly brought up to their trade from birth, for when they were but babes in arms they were taken up to dizzy heights by their steeplejack brothers. They could climb almost before they could walk, and now are as efficient steeplejacks as are to be found anywhere in the country.

THEY`RE BRITAINS ONLY "STEEPLEJILLS"

From " The Peoples" Correspondant.

The claim to be Britains only "Steeplejills" is made by two pretty Midlands Sisters aged seventeen and nineteen.

These steeplejills were truly brought up to their trade from birth, for when they were but babes in arms they were taken up to dizzy heights by their steeplejack brothers. They could climb almost before they could walk, and now are as efficient steeplejacks as are to be found anywhere in the country.

****

LEICESTER YOUNG WOWANS REMARKABLE PLUCK

The inhabitants of Swithland and district had, on Thursday afternoon the opportunity of witnessing an exciting and dangerous climb by a young lady of the name Miss Lydia Akiens, aged 15 years, who lives at 39, Newington Street, Shaftsbury Avenue.

Mr J. T. Akiens, the girls father, is at present employed in the construction of a chimney at the Leicester Corporation Waterworks, at Swithland. The erection is 144 feet high, and is used by the engines which pump purified water from the Swithland Reservoir to the Highfields and Stoneygate districts.

The young lady ascended the chimney on Thursday afternoon on the outside by ladders, round waist being attached a leather strap, to which was fastened a hook, enabling her to rest when tired by hanging the hook to the ladder. The ascent was made in about 5 minutes, and Miss Akiens then coolly proceeded to take a walk round the scaffolding surrounding the top of the chimney. After spending about half an hour in this "eyrie" she came down, occupying even less time in descending than she did in ascending.

Miss Akiens who is 5ft. 2in in height, on Wednesday ascended a chimney at the Leicester Gas Works, near the Belgrave road, with just as much ease. Her father challenges the female world under 18 years of age, that his daughter will climb the highest chimncys and steeples with any comer, he to have the fixing and providing of the apparatus.

****

The chimney that great granddad built on the left, the Swithland`s Leicester Corporation Waterworks and the Leicester Gasworks in Belgrave on the right. The two chimneys Lydia climbed in one week.

J.T.Akiens junior , Lydia, and J.T.Akiens great granddad taking the old Belgrave pumping station chimney down by chopping out a section of the base, a "doorway", before dropping it. The article below was written 45 years later. Hard graft with walls that thick and no power tools. A very risky business, the chimney could drop at any moment. The canes were there to show them when it was ready to fall giving them time to get out of the way. Many steeplejacks were killed by falling masonry and chimneys falling on them because of this method of taking them down.

Camera Looks Back

The Felling Of A Be!grave Chimney : THIS week the camera looks back 45 years ... on a piece of Akiens family history, the felling of the 90-foot chimney stack at the old Belgrave Pumping Station. Several members of the family took part in what a local newspaper called "a smart piece of work." They included "the famous lady steeplejack Miss Lydia Akiens."

Also in the picture are Mr. J. T. Akiens father, Baden, Jesse, Tom and Harold. This is how the felling of the chimney was described by the local paper: "At about two o'clock on Wednesday afternoon, after working five hours, Mr. Akiens gave the signal . . . "The workers made off to a safe distance and the stack crashed down- only a foot from the estimated place marked." A very smart piece of work.

The chimney at Belgraves Abbey pumping station, where dad told us Dracula lived. 150 foot tall give or take a few feet. Dad said it was a baby compared to some of the ones they worked on. Like the ones in the next pictures.

A monster of a chimney, well over 300 foot tall. The one below being dropped somewhere in Cornwall. There would have been close to a million bricks in this chimney, and it weighed several thousand tonnes.

A chimney of similar size to this was estimated to have enough bricks in it to build 38 medium sized villas. A lot of the reclaimed bricks from these demolished chimneys were used for that. Very profitable for the family.

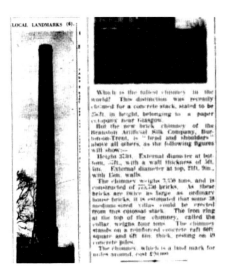

Which is the tallest chimney in the world ? This distinction was recently claimed for a concrete stack, stated to ne 250ft. in height, belonging to a paper company near Glasgow. (There were much taller chimneys around at that time so I don't know who did the research for this newspaper) But the new brick chimney of the Branston Artificial Silk Company, Burton-on-Trent, is head and shoulders above all others, as the following figures will show :-

Height 373ft. External diameter at bottom 35 ft., with a wall thickness of 5 feet 5in. External diameter at the top , 21 feet 9 in. walls

The chimney weighs 3,450 tonnes and is constructed of 775,750 bricks. As these bricks are twice as large as ordinary house bricks, it is estimated that some 38 medium sized villas could be erected from this colossal stack. The iron ring at the top, called the collar, weighs four tons. The chimney stands on a reinforced concrete raft 60 feet square and 6ft. 6 in. thick resting on 49 concrete piles. The chimney which is a landmark for miles around, cost £50,000.

* * * * * * * * * * * * * * * *

The iron ring weighed four ton. That's like 3 mini coopers on the top of the chimney. Imagine having to take that down when it came to demolishing it.

An unknown steeplejack wrote in to this newspaper, highlighting the dangers they faced. The wealthy mill and factory owners would let the chimneys rot, sooner than spend a few quid sorting them. They were directly responsible in some cases for the deaths that occurred. But I haven't come across any newspaper reports of any of them ever getting prosecuted for the deaths of people they employed, They were even ridiculed for it in cartoons.

STEEPLEJACKS DANGER.

TO THE EDITOR OF THE STANDARD.

Sir,— l read in your issue of yesterday that another steeplejack has been killed, this time at Bolton, by the coping chimney head giving way. This has been a terrible year for steeplejacks. Hardly a week passes that does not record a steeplejack's death, sometimes two being hurled together. In a few cases it is due to steeplejacks' contempt for danger, but in the majority of cases due solely to owners allowing the chimneys to fall into such a state that for their own safety they are compelled to employ a steeplejack. The result is that as soon as a chimney is laddered" the climber steps on to the lop. and, before he has any warning, the brickwork collapse. It is quite time that chimney owners should be compelled to have their chimneys periodically examined, thus reducing the yearly death toll by one half.
.   I am Sir, vour obedient servant,

Dec 8.   STEEPLEJACK.

****

An earthquake struck East Anglia in 1884, dozens of chimneys fell like dominoes causing destruction on a massive scale.

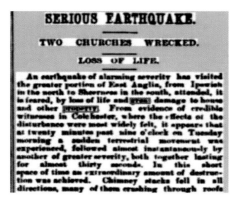

SERIOUS EARTHQUAKE.

TWO CHURCHES WRECKED.   LOSS OF LIFE.

An earthquake of alarming severity has visited the greater portion of East Anglia, from Ipswich in the north to Sheerness in the south, attended , it is feared, by loss of life and great damage to house and other property.

From evidence of credible witnesses in Colchester, where the effects of the disturbance were most widely felt, it appears that at twenty minutes past nine o`clock on Tuesday morning a sudden terrestrial movement was experienced, followed by another of greater severity, both together lasting almost thirty seconds. In this short space of time an extraordinary amount of destruction was achieved. Chimney stacks fell in all directions, many of them crashing through roofs...

＊＊＊＊＊＊＊＊＊＊＊＊＊＊＊

A chimney fell onto a factory in Bradford in 1883, killing 54 people and injuring 25 others. It happened as a direct result of the owners wanting it built on the cheap, changing the plans to cut costs, going against everything the chimney builders advised. When it came down it didn`t collapse without warning. For weeks it was seen swaying badly in the wind. The work steeplejacks did prevented these sort of tragedies happening. That`s how important their work was.

THE BRADFORD CHIMNEY DISASTER.

INQUEST.

The inquiry into the circumstances attending the death of the 54 persons killed by the fall of the chimney at Newlands Mill, Bradford, on the 28th December was

THE BRADFORD CHIMNEY DISASTER.   INQUEST

The inquiry into the circumstances attending the deaths of the 54 persons killed by the fall of the chimney at Newlands Mill Bradford on the 28th December was resumed yesterday, and important evidence was given by Mr. William Moulson, one of the contractors who built the chimney.

EVIDENCE BY THE CONTRACTOR:

It appeared that the foundations were laid in a short disused coal shaft. This was widened, and five concrete pits were sunk through the coal bed to a stratum of shale. For some distance around the old workings were packed with rough rubble work. When, however, the chimney had been built ten yards high, Sir Henry' Ripley, who had given verbal directions to the contractor, instead of getting specifications prepared, caused the plans to be altered, putting ornamental sunk panels into the facing work.

The contractors spoke strongly against the proposal, as a great source of weakness, but Mr. Ripley grinned, and said " You must do it my way." It was suggested to him also, that the interior masonry was not strong enough, and he consented to the addition of nine inches of brickwork up to a certain height, but to the abolition of rubble work which he and others deemed secure. The witness, who spoke slightingly of the mode of straightening the chimney, was still being examined when the inquiry was adjourned.

****

82

I wonder if that arsehole Sir Henry Ripley was still grinning, when he ended up in court over all those deaths, thats if he ended up in court. Four cottages were destroyed and 70 men were put out of work when a chimney fell, during another storm in Sheffield. The damage was widespread across the city.

> of which was of gold.
> The Bank Dyeworks, Ashton-road, in the occupation
> of Mr. Henry Crabtree, have been completely stopped,
> through the falling of their large chimney during the
> storm; and four cottages were destroyed by the chimney
> in its fall These works usually employ about 70 men.

The Bank Dyeworks, Ashton road, in the occupation of Mr. Henry Crabtree, have been completely stopped through the falling of their large chimney during the storm, and four cottages were destroyed by the chimney in its fall. These works usually employ about 70 men…

****

These accidents could have all been avoided, if the factory owners weren`t so tight fisted. Time and again these rotting chimneys fell but they didn`t listen, they weren`t bothered enough to do anything about it, even when they were clearly told the chimneys were dangerous. Like this newspaper below reported, the chimney was rotten from top to bottom.

THE BURNLEY CHIMNEY DISASTER.

GRAVE ALLEGATIONS.

> At Burnley to-day an inquest was held on the
> three victims of the recent chimney disaster.
> Witnesses, including the occupiers of the shops ad-
> joining, gave evidence as to the dangerous condition
> of the structure, and the complaints made to the
> owner, a woman. The coroner remarked that there
> was no doubt the chimney was rotten from top to
> bottom. A steeplejack deposed that he had
> noticed that the chimney was rotten, and had
> offered to tender to pull it down. The ex-Borough

THE BURNLEY CHIMNEY DISASTER

GRAVE ALLEGATIONS

At Burnley to-day an inquest was held on the three victims of the recent chimney disaster. Witnesses, including the occupiers of the shops adjoining, gave evidence as to the dangerous condition of the structure, and the complaints made to the owner, a woman. The coroner remarked that there was no doubt the chimney was rotten from top to bottom. A steeplejack deposed that he had noticed that the chimney was rotten and had offered a tender to pull it down.

****

In the next article a thousand people were made unemployed when this chimney collapsed, and steeplejacks were killed. A real tragedy for the surrounding community and the families of the steeplejacks who lost their sons, brothers, husbands and fathers.

STEEPLEJACKS KILLED.
A number of steeplejacks had a shocking experience on Wednesday at Bridge Mills, Tintwistle, near Manchester. The main building of the mill was recently destroyed. The damage amounting to nearly £50,000, while over a thousand cotton operatives were thrown out of employment. While the the steeplejacks were engaged in demolishing the old walls, several tons of stonework fell in, cras-

STEEPLEJACKS KILLED

A number of Steeplejacks had a shocking experience on Wednesday at Bridge Mills, Tintwistle, near Manchester. The main building of the mill was recently destroyed. The damage amounting to nearly £50,000, while over a thousand cotton operatives were thrown out of employment. While the steeplejacks were engaged in demolishing the old walls, several tons of stonework fell in, crashing through several floor of the factory.

****

84

Very young children were killed and badly injured when a chimney collapsed on to a school.

THE LOW MOOR CHIMNEY DISASTER

The inquests on the bodies of the infant victims of this disaster were held yesterday, the first on the body of...

****

Fatal Fall of a Chimney.

A terrible disaster occurred at Cleckheaton, near Bradford, by which 12 persons have been killed and several others have been injured, some of them fatally. At ten minutes to five o'clock a factory chimney fell upon a spinning and weaving shed, occupied by Mr. Wesley Barraclough. Nearly 60 persons were at work in the building at the time. The chimney crashed down upon the structure and demolished more than one-half of it. Nearly 30 per-

sons, chiefly girls, were either buried beneath the many tons of debris or escaped in a marvellous manner. The Cleckheaton Fire Brigade, from a neighbouring mill, was soon on the spot, with a large corps of volunteer workers, and, under the superintendence of the police, the work of rescuing the living and removing the dead was soon begun. As the night wore on the scene inside the mill, which had been partially destroyed, lost none of its interest. By the light of lanterns some hundred persons were busily at work removing the tons of ruins which still apparently covered five persons. Strong ropes were made fast to huge iron girders, and large numbers of men slowly removed these impediments to the work of rescue. The chimney was built some fifty years ago, and was sixty yards high. It was of brick, and at the time of the

Fatal Fall of a Chimney

A terrible disaster occurred at Cleckheaton, near Bradford, by which' 12 persons have been killed and several others have been injured, some of them fatally. At ten minutes to five o'clock a factory chimney fell upon a spinning and weaving shed, occupied by Mr. Wesley Barraclough. Nearly 60 persons were at work in the building at the time. The chimney crashed down upon the structure and demolished more than one half of it. Nearly 30 per-

-sons, chiefly girls, were either buried beneath the many tonnes of debris or escaped n a marvellous manner. The Cleckheaton Fire Brigade, from a neighbouring mill was soon on the spot, with a large corps of volunteer workers, and under the superintendence of the police, the work of rescuing the living and removing the dead was soon begun. As the night wore on the scene inside the mill, which had been partially destroyed, lost none of its interest. By the light of lanterns some hundred persons were busily at work removing the tons of ruins which still apparently covered five persons. Strong ropes were made fast to huge iron girders, and large numbers of men slowly removed these impediments to the work of rescue. The chimney was built some fifty years ago, and was sixty yards high. It was of brick and at the time of the ....

****

Another kind of job they did was straighten chimneys. They would lean probably as much as 3 or 4 feet out of plumb at the top, usually due to water getting in the foundations, or being built on mined coal beds was also another reason in some cases. This wasn't a job my dad ever did, it was before his time, but granddad did when he was young.

A Problem for an Engineer.

86

One of the most perilous undertakings ever undertaken by a steeplejack was the straightening of a large chimney stack, 200 feet high. It was as much as 4 feet 6 inches out of plumb. Now, the reason for the listing was not through faulty construction, because the chimney itself was in sound condition, but the foundation, had subsided on one side, causing the chimney to heel. I may tell you when a chimney deviates as much as four and a half feet from the perpendicular it a serious matter.

He conquered the problem by removing a course of bricks for about two thirds of the circumference and inserting iron wedges temporarily in their place. No fewer than four courses were thus removed, and then came the crucial moment when the wedges were one by one withdrawn and a thinner course of bricks inserted.- Slowly and steadily the whole chimney, a thousand tons in weight, sank back into the perpendicular without the fracture of a single brick outside the lines of cutting.

****

The chimney before and after the work was done, and the work in progress.

If a chimney was going to subside, it usually did so within a few years of being built as it settled on the ground it was built on. There weren`t many, if any chimneys being built around the time dad was born. Electricity from the power stations was replacing steam by then. They tackled these tricky jobs by chopping out a course of bricks going half way round the chimney, on the opposite side to where it was leaning, and they would hammer long steel wedges into the brickwork. Im not entirely sure how it all worked, im just going from memory of what i was told years ago. A thinner course of bricks would be inserted, and somehow the stack would then settle straighter when they removed the wedges. The process would be repeated a couple of feet higher up if needed. A very risky job with hundreds of tons of bricks shifting above them. An extremely essential job, these chimneys would undoubtedly topple over if left.

This was another chimney they dropped in Exeter in 1912. The photo on the right is after they rebuilt it. They worked all over the country, travelling by horse and cart in those days. When granddad was a young lad they bought their first truck for the business. There were loads of stories that passed down through the family that didn't make the newspapers. Stories that were as hard to believe, as some of those that did get published.

The family have lived in Belgrave in Leicester, since before records began in 1600. It was supposedly originally called Bel Grave, two words, after a giant called Bel died there, from an old folklore tale. Belgrave was also known as Dummy town. Whenever the police turned up asking questions, everyone turned into dummies. No one had seen or heard anything at all. There is another story that says it was because someone hung a dummy from a lamppost, outside the Bulls head I think. I prefer to believe the first reason.

It was in one of these fields men used to gamble all their wages away, and of course the police often raided the game. As a boy I was often a look out for the gambling school. I would hide in the hedge and if I saw the police I would give a whistle – a warning to the men – and they would all run as fast as they could to prevent being arrested for playing Pitch and Toss. One Friday evening a police inspector came and he shouted "At last I've caught you!" but, much to his surprise, the men picked him up and threw him in the river! Later when the police came round asking questions to find out the identity of the culprits no one knew anything and that's how Belgrave came to have the name Dummy Town. But believe me folk weren't so dumb in Dummy Town, they were very loyal to each other. Belgrave people would fight amongst themselves, but if anyone outside of Belgrave started anything heaven help them, the Belgrave Boys would soon sort them out!

Belgrave was full of interesting characters and there were loads of memorable families. I often read about some of them told by their families today, on the facebook group *Bygone Belgrave.* Its a wealth of information, seeing photos and reading stories about the people who lived there and the buildings that are long gone. If any of these families would like to put their families stories together in a book like I have, for their future generations, id be only too happy to help with that. Its surprisingly easy to do.

Because the family have lived in Belgrave for so long theres a very good chance we are related to many of these families somewhere in the past. If anyone in Belgrave, or Leicester has any of these names in their family histories, we could be related. A lot of Belgrave people were moved out of the area to places like Stocking Farm, New Parks, Braunstone, Eyres Monsell, Mowmacre, Saffron Lane, because of the slum clearance programs of the 1960`s and 70`s. These are the maiden names of the women who have married into our family, in my direct line going back to 1600. The names are :- Collins, Turner, Cobley, Goodfellow, Taylor, Frazier, Dawson, Taylor, Houghton, Thacker, Gibson, Cockrane, Cursley, Herbert and Pedge.

William b.13 April 1600, d.4 December 1651 — m. 18 September 1600 — **Anna Collins** b.14 June 1601, d.18 September 1661

Thomas b.3 July 1622, d.1 January 1677 — m. 19 August 1641 — **Mary Turner** b.8 March 1622, d.10 July 1688

John b.19 August 1643, d.1 June 1698 — m. 9 December 1663 — **Ann Cobley** b.3 July 1644, d.23 February 1704

Thomas b.3 August 1664, d.19 March 1720 — m. 3 July 1683 — **Mary Goodfellow** b.18 October 1664, d.14 September 1736

John b.3 July 1685, d.1 June 1740 — m. 13 September 1705 — **Sarah Taylor** b.4 September 1686, d.23 December 1749

William b.2 March 1700, d.18 May 1760 — m. 28 August 1725 — **Mary Frazier** b.9 December 1706, d.10 February 1763

William b.10 March 1725, d.1 August 1777 — m. 13 June 1744 — **Elizabeth Dawson** b.23 June 1725, d.17 March 1787

William b.2 June 1748, d.27 January 1810 — m. 18 May 1769 — **Mary Ann Taylor** b.12 August 1748, d.19 March 1790

Thomas b.4 September 1768, d.18 April 1838 — m. 15 July 1792 — **Sarah Ann Houghton** b.14 August 1769, d.16 June 1829

John b.22 February 1795, d.3 July 1845 — m. 4 September 1816 — **Susanah Thacker** b.1799 Market Harborough, d.13 July 1855

John b.5 January 1819, d.4 June 1869 — m. 19 February 1838 — **Sarah Gibson** b.12 March 1820, d.9 May 1873

John Thomas b.3 December 1839, d.10 July 1881 — m. 1860 — **Caroline Cockrane** b.19 August 1841, d.

John Thomas b.5 March 1864, d.5 July 1931 — m. 15 November 1884 — **Ellen Cursley** b.1 December 1863, d.

There will be hundreds more men and women who married into the family, because each of these generations had several brothers and sisters. Some of the names who have married into the family not in a direct line, that I know of are, Bhatia, Melbourne, Niland, Coles, Suffolk, Goodwin, to name just a few.

Belgrave was a very tight knit community, it was possibly the roughest area of Leicester back then. If anyone came looking for trouble, the local lads sorted them all out. In great granddads day the pubs had sawdust on the floors to soak up any spilt beer, or blood. In those days disagreements were usually resolved between men by going outside and having a one on one punch up. When one man was down on the ground the fight was over. Then they both went back in the pub and had a drink together, the loser paying. That kind of violence was much more common and acceptable back then. They wouldn`t dream of kicking a man in the head. Well, the men wouldn`t.

Granddad was always getting into fights outside pubs in the Belgrave area, he loved it, because he was good at it. Like anything, we often enjoy doing what we are good at, whatever it is. He told me he had quite a few free pints. When i spoke to some of the old Belgrave people about the family when i was researching this, some were a bit confused when i asked them if they knew my Granddad Sid Akiens. Because there were quite a few of the family living in the area back then. When i told them Granddad had a thumb and two fingers missing, they knew exactly who i meant.

All the family have been born there since before records began in 1600. As far as im aware all the family in my line have been married at St Peters, Belgrave. Dad was proud of where he came from, that he was a Belgruff boy, as he would pronounce it, like a lot of locals did, and still do.

Below is part of the professionally researched family tree. Three generations died in 1931, son, father and grandfather, all of them had the same name.

As you can see from the family tree, the AKIENS family have resided in the Belgrave area for the past 400 years. Most of the men have either been labourers, brickmakers and bricklayers, and steeplejacks.

The name AKIENS has changed over the years. In 1600 it was spelt ALfINS (the f becoming a k). In 1670, it changed to AKINES and in 1730, it then changed to AIKENS. From 1780, it changed to its present form AKIENS.

1931 was a year of tradegy for the Akiens family. Three generations of the family grandfather, son and grandson all died tragically in the same year. John Thomas, grandson of John Thomas Akiens and Caroline Cochrane, died in a motor accident.

On the 5th July 1931, John Thomas Akiens, born 5th March 1864, son of John Thomas Akiens and Caroline Cochrane, died unexpectedly. At the time he was living at 25 Dayne Street, Leicester. The funeral was stopped by the police, following allegations of poisoning, made by his brother-in-law, Walter Allen. The post mortem revealed death by natural causes. He was buried on the 9th July 1931 at Welford Road Cemetery, Leicester.

The following day on the 10th July 1931, his father John Thomas Akiens (husband of Caroline Cochrane), born 3rd December 1839 and then aged 92 years, hung himself.

"As you can see from the family tree, the Akiens have resided in the Belgrave area for the past 400 years. Most of the men have been either labourers, brickmakers, bricklayers and steeplejacks.

The name AKIENS has changed over the years. In 1600 it was spelt ALFINS, (the f becoming a K). In 1670 it changed to AKINES and in 1730 it then changed to AIKENS, from 1780 it changed to its present form AKIENS.

1931 was a year of tragedy for the Akiens family. Three generations of the family, grandfather , son and grandson all died tragically in the same year. John Thomas grandson of John Thomas Akiens and Caroline Cockrane, died in a motor accident.

On the 5th of July1931, John Thomas Akiens born 5th March 1864, son of John Thomas Akiens and Caroline Cockrane, (Husband of Ellen Cursely) died unexpectedly. At the time he was living at 25 Payne street Leicester. The funeral was stopped by the police following allegations of poisoning, made by his brother in law Walter Allen.

The post mortem revealed death by natural causes. He was Buried on the 9th July 1931 at Welford road cemetery.

The following day on the 10th of July his father, John Thomas Akiens (Husband of Caroline Cockrane,) born December 3rd 1839, and then aged 92 years, hung himself."

$$* * * * * * * * * * * * * * * * *$$

I don`t know much about Great great granddad John Thomas Akiens born 3$^{rd}$ December 1839. I`ve never even seen a photo of him. Granddad said that he had one hell of a temper. Everyone stayed out of his way when he was pissed off. I know he hung himself using the ropes that helped make the families modest fortune, the day after his sons funeral. These two newspapers from the 1870`s show he was no stranger to getting into bother.

Below is one story the papers wrote about him and great great grandma in 1874, getting into bother in the Telegraph Inn, a Belgrave pub that was demolished years ago. Someone clouted great great grandma, giving her two black eyes. So great great granddad knocked him out, then she kicked him in the head while he was out cold on the ground. It was probably just a typical night out in Belgrave at the time, it was a rough place to live.

92

Edward Warner was charged with assaulting Caroline Akiens-
Complainant said she was the Wife of John Thomas Akiens. About ten
o`clock on the night of 21st, she went with her husband into the Telegraph inn,
Belgrave gate, fer a pint of ale. Defendant came in and was quarrelsome, when
the landlord put him out. Complainant went out soon after, and on getting to
the door the defendant was there, and he struck her a violent blow between the
eyes, which knocked her down. Both eyes were blackened. She was picked up
and was taken to her sisters, opposite- Elizabeth Frost, who picked the
complainant up, corroborated.

Defendant denied the assault in toto and called a girl named Mary Ann Taylor,
who said about ten o`clock on the night in question, she was passing the
Telegraph inn, when she saw the defendant come out. Complainants husband
struck the defendant and knocked him out, upon which the complainant went
up and kicked him in the mouth. Complainant then rushed into a crowd, and a
tall man struck her in the face; it did not knock her down- Thomas Gansey
gave similar evidence, but defendant was fines 21s, or 14 days imprisonment.

****

93

Bench made an order for 8s. a week.

UNPROVOKED ASSAULT.—John Thomas Akiens, Belper-street, was charged with assaulting John Thomas Booker, on December 9th.—Complainant stated that, without any provocation, defendant struck him in his face, and afterwards chased him down the street.—Defendant said he did not know anything about it, as he was drunk. He had been previously convicted of assault, and the Bench fined him 40s., or a month's imprisonment.

UNPROVED ASSAULT.- Mr J. T. Akiens bricklayer, Belper street, was charged with assaulting John Thomas Booker, December 9th.-Complainant stated that without any provocation, defendant struck him twice in the face, and afterwards chased him down the street.- Defendant said he did not know anything about it, as he was drunk. He had been previously convicted of assault, and the bench fined him 40`s or a months imprisonment.

****

John Thomas Aikens, of 113, Belper Street, steeplejack, was charged with assaulting his sister-in-law, Gertrude Aikens, on the 14th inst. It appeared that the defendant was the worse for drink, and he started a quarrel with complainant's husband. When she tried to part them defendant struck her on the head. —Fined 10s., or seven days' hard labour.

John Thomas Akiens, of 113 Belper Street, steeplejack, was charged with assaulting his Sister-in-law, Gertrude Akiens, on the 14th inst. It appeared that the defendant was the worse for drink, and he started a quarrel with complainant`s husband. When she tried to part them defendant struck her on the head.

Fined 10s, or seven days hard labour.

****

While researching the sort of work the family did online, i read literally thousands of newspaper stories all about steeplejacks. When Fred Dibnah said they were mad in the old days, he wasn`t kidding when you hear about some of the stuff they got up to

A good few of them i read about were cat burglars, lead thieves, con men, bigamists, numerous articles on assaults and fights, countless drunk and disorderlies, speeding convictions, they were up court for all sorts of reasons. A couple of them in the articles below were using gelignite and nitro glycerine meant for demolishing chimneys, to blow safes. The articles below have nothing to do with the family.

THE DYNAMITE PLOTS.

SEIZURE OF EXPLOSIVES AT LEICESTER.

The Leicester police have made a seizure of nitro glycerine in a gelatinised condition, in thirty-five packages in a garden on the Freeman's Common; and a steeple jack named William Mitchell has been taken into custody

DYNAMITE PLOTS

SEIZURE OF EXPLOSIVES AT LEICESTER

The Leicester Police have made a seizure of Nitro Glicerine in a gelatinised condition, in thirty five packages in a garden on the Freemans common, and a steeplejack named William Mitchell has been taken into custody.

****

HEAVY SENTENCES PASSED.

An amazing story was told at the Old Bailey, London, of how cinemas were broken into and safes blown open with gelignite when seven men were sentenced on charges to which they pleaded guilty relating to breaking into cinemas and stealing property and cash.

.Robert Manderson (24), steeplejack

HEAVY SENTENCES PASSED

An amazing story was told at the old Bailey. London, of how cinemas were broken into and safes blown open with Gelignite when seven men were sentenced on charges to which they pleaded guilty relating to breaking into cinemas and stealing property and cash.

Robert Manderson , (24) Steeplejack….

****

95

During the war the Germans even had a steeplejack spy, who looked down on the goings on in London. He got deported. The hair brained scheme he had in mind they probably should have committed the nutter.

Carl Fincu, the German steeplejack, alleged to possess plans of a "land mine" for the annihilation of the British Army, has been

One of them was a train robber.

MISSING BOX OF SILVER.
FOUR-YEAR-OLD THEFT RECALLED.

STEEPLEJACK'S PLEA OF GUILTY.

The alleged robbery of £800 in silver coin from a Great Northern Railway train

Some were even murderers, many of them were a law unto themselves. They make my family look like saints, some of them.

DEATH SENTENCE ON STEEPLEJACK.

FATAL STAB DURING QUARREL.

Sentenced to death at Manchester Assizes yesterday, Francis Hyland, steeplejack, Red Bank, was recommended to mercy by the jury on the ground that when he fatally stabbed William Rothwell, a motor driver, he was drunk.

Following a quarrel about war service in a Manchester public-house, Hyland, who had consumed over twenty pints of beer during the day and night, stabbed Rothwell from behind with a jack knife.

In the witness-box prisoner said he remembered nothing of the affair but his arrival at the police station. He admitted having spent pension and dole money on drink.

DEATH SENTENCE ON STEEPLEJACK.

96

FATAL STAB DURING QUARREL.

Sentenced to death at Manchester Assizes yesterday, Francis Hyland, steeplejack, Red Bank, was recommended to mercy the jury on the ground that when he fatally stabbed William Rothwell. a motor driver, he was drunk. Following a quarrel about war service a Manchester public-house, Hyland, who had consumed over twenty pints of beer during the day and night, stabbed Rothwell from behind with jack knife. In the witness-box prisoner_ said he remembered nothing of the affair, but his arrival the police station. He admitted having spent pension and dole money on drink.

****

One even put a brick through the Prime Ministers windows.

THE PREMIER'S WINDOWS.

At Bow-street Mr. Graham Campbell imposed fines of 20s. each and the damages on Lucy Wilson and Joseph Conway, the latter described as a steeplejack, charged with breaking windows yesterday at the Prime Minister's official residence in Downing-street.

Even though the family were a rough lot who had more than their share of getting into trouble, in the courts, fighting or whatever, they would do anything to help anyone. They used to make sure the war widows around Belgrave had coal for their fires in winter and enough food. Most people were like that back then, there was a real community spirit. They did so many things for charity, like raising money for the soup kitchens, for orphans to go on holiday to Mablethorpe or contributing to the war effort in some way.

Great granddad John Thomas Akiens, Born 5th March 1864. He broke nearly every bone in his body during his sixty plus years climbing. He was at one time the head of the R.A.O.B freemasons.

The Royal Antedeluvian Order of Buffaloes. He was knight director of ceremonies. K.O.M, D.P.G.P, P.P.C.C. Whatever all that means. He founded his own lodge which still exists today, the Arthur Coles lodge. Lydia Akiens his daughter married a man named Coles so i presume it was named that because of him or one of his relatives. I visited them where they still have their lodge meetings today, in a pub just off Fosse road in Leicester.

They gave me a copy of all the minutes from meetings they had when he was the grand primo of the order in 1926. I couldn`t make head or tail of it, it was like it was written in some sort of code. They told me that during WW1, every member of the organisation donated one penny to the war effort. There were that many members they bought 11 ambulances.

This is his membership certificate from 1915. A lot of the family joined the Buffaloes over the years.

They had judges, solicitors, politicians, all kinds of very influential people in the order. It was quite unusual for a working class man to make it to the position of Grande Primo knight of the order.

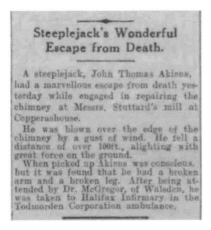

Steeplejacks Wonderful Escape From Death

A steeplejack named John Thomas Akiens, had a marvellous escape from death yesterday while engaged in repairing the chimney at Messrs. Stuttards mill at Copperhouse.

He was blown over the edge of the chimney by a gust of wind. He fell a distance of over 100 ft., alighting with great force on the ground.

When picked up Akiens was conscious, but it was found that he had a broken arm and broken leg. After being attended dy Dr. Mcgregor, of Walsden, he was taken to Halifax infirmary in the Todmorden Corporation ambulance.

****

Another story well known in the family, was that great granddad had a fight with his brother Samuel on Victoria road north. At the back of where the Jungle club now stands, back then it was the old Belgrave Working Mens Club. Samuel brought a sword to the fight and great granddad fought bare knuckle. Samuel lost. I haven`t come across that story in any of the papers from that time, but enough people in the family were told and remember that story, so im fairly sure it happened. I did however come across this next newspaper report. It certainly shows a couple of things, that there was bad blood between them, and that Samuel was more than ready to use a sword. Im inclined to believe the court case wasn`t the end of the matter.

Labourer's Strange Behaviour.—Saml. Akiens (37), labourer, 48, Evans-road, was charged, on remand, with behaving in a disorderly manner in Victoria-road North on October 3. He was also charged with threatening his brother, John Thomas Akiens, on the same date.—This charge had also been adjourned from October 4 in order that defendant's mental condition might be inquired into.—The evidence given last week was to the effect that defendant went to his brother's house and threatened him with a sword without any provocation.—Defendant's wife now said that she believed her husband would

Labourer`s Strange Behaviour.-

100

Samuel Akiens (37) labourer, of 48 Evans road, was charged on remand, with behaving in a disorderly manner in Victoria road North on October 3rd. He was also charged with threatening his brother, John Thomas Akiens, on the same date. This charge had also been adjourned from October 4th in order that defendant's mental condition might be inquired into. The evidence given last week was to effect that defendant went to his brother`s house and threatened him with a sword without any provocation. - Defendants wife now said she believed her husband would....

****

Great granddads brothers worked with him steeplejacking, but he financed Samuel in a haulage company which failed. Samuel had been in and out of prison a number of times prior to this happening.

I don`t know if that was the reason for them to have such a bad fall out that it came to that. Apparrently Samuel was transported to Canada to split the pair up after the sword / fist fight, because they were so bad. Granddad always maintained he didn`t emigrate as the family tree says. He became quite a leading figure in the mounties, the Canadian Mounted police, allegedly, but iv found no proof of that. Iv no idea what actually happened to him.

The next is another article mentioning the family being famous for their work.

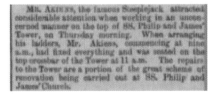

Mr Akiens the famous steeplejack, attracted considerable attention when working in an unconcerned manner at the top of SS. Phillip and James tower, on Thursday morning. When arranging his ladders, Mr Akiens, commencing at 9 a.m, had fixed everything and was seated on the top crossbar of the tower at 11 a.m. The repairs to the tower are a portion of the great scheme of renovation being carried out at SS Phillip and James church.

****

He saved a childs life who fell in the Belgrave locks at the bottom of Holden street in 1904. He didn't piss about, he just dived in and got the lad out. He was breathing but unconscious. Having done his St. Johns ambulance training he knew how to resuscitate the young lad.

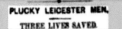

PLUCKY LEICESTER MEN

THREE LIVES SAVED

The watch committee of the corporation on Tuesday evening had the pleasant duty to perform in commending three persons for their courage and resource in saving life. The men thus honoured were Mr. George Henry Issitt, an insurance agent, Mr John T. Akiens, a builder and steeple climber of 16 Down street, and Mr Herbert Treahearn, a Labourer of 26 Vann street.

The rescue by Mr John T. Akiens, was under similar circumstances as the first. A boy named Harold Hollidge, aged eight, living with his parents at 33, Lee street, was playing on the canal lock gates near Holden street Belgrave, when he slipped and fell into the water in the lock. Mr Akiens did not witness the accident, but he heard a little girl cry out there was a boy in the lock.

He ran to the spot and saw a man trying to reach the boy with a fishing rod. Mr Akiens dived into the lock, brought the boy to the side, and handed him to some men on the towing path. They then pulled Mr Akiens out, and he went to the boy. The latter was unconscious but his rescuer completed his good work by reviving the boy by means of artificial respiration, afterwards taking him to his (Mr Akiens) home , where he was cared for until he arrival of the boys parents, who took him away. The water in the lock was at least 10 feet deep. The committee handed Mr Akiens a copy of a resolution they had passed. with 10s 6d, to cover the cost of the soiled trousers.

****

It`s not the only time he saved someone from drowning, it happened again in St Helens where they were based in the north. They missed his first name out in the newspaper but it was him.

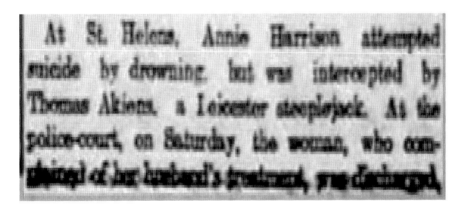

At St. Helens, Annie Harrison attempted suicide by drowning, but was intercepted by Thomas Akiens, a Leicester steeplejack. At the police-court on Saturday, the woman, who complained of her husband`s treatment, was discharged.

****

In this next article above Grt Granddad was up court again in Cheriton Bishop. Great granddad lost, he had to pay the bloke a couple of quid in old money.

103

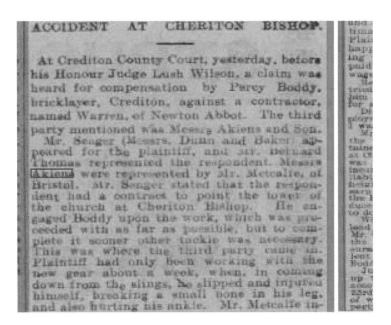

1914 : ACCIDENT AT CHERITON BISHOP.

At Crediton county court yesterday, before his honour Judge Lush Wilson, a claim was heard for compensation by Percy Boddy, bricklayer, Crediton, against a contractor named Warren of Newton Abbot. The Third party mentioned was Messrs. Akiens and Son. Mr Seager (Messrs. Dunn and Baker) appeared for the plaintiff, and Mr. Bernard Thomas represented the respondant. Messrs Akiens were represented by Mr. Metcalfe of Bristol. Mr Seager stated that the respondant had a contract to point the tower of the church at Cheriton Bishop. He engaged Boddy upon the work, which was preceeded with as far as possible, but to complete it sooner other tackle was neccessary. This was where the third party came in. Plaintiff had only been working with the new gear about a week, when, in coming down for the slings, he slipped and injured himself, breaking a small bone in his leg, and also hurting his ankle. Mr Metcalfe intimated that the accident was admitted. Plaintiff, giving evidence, said the accident happened on june 23rd. The work of pointing was done by means of slings. He was paid 7d per hour, and, with overtime, his wages amounted to 36s a week.

Replying to Mr. Metcalfe, witness said he tried to get work after the doctor signed him off the club but was unable to do so for about three weeks.

Did you try to get work at your old employers ? My solicitor let Mr. Warren know i was able do light work.

Mr Thomas : There was a sub contract with the third party, Mr Akiens. Respondent obtained a contract to do repairs at Cheriton Bishop, the principal part of which was the pointing of the tower. He found his insurance policy would not cover him for the liability to the workmen above a certain height, and also he had not the tackle necessary for the work. He made inquiries from the Exeter brick and tile company, who introduced him to Mr. Akiens and Mr Akiens agreed to do that part of the work.

William Warren said Mr Akiens agreed to lend him the tackle and help him in the work. Mr Akiens was to lend him the tackle, superintend the work, and became responsible for the insurance for a certain sum per hour. Witness lent Mr Boddy to Mr Akiens but did not inform Boddy of that fact.

Judgement was entered for 14s 4 1/2d a week up to September 23rd, Less £4 10s paid on account. Also 3s per week since September 23rd in view of plaintiffs now reduced rate of wages. Costs on scale B. Costs for third party on scale B.

****

When grt granddad died in 1931 his estate was worth several thousand pounds. Ten years later you could buy a semi detached house in a nice area for around £250. By that reckoning in todays money it would probably be a 6 or 7 figure sum i`m sure. I have no idea where all the money went. It was gone long before i was born, before my dad was born.

They made money twice on a lot of jobs, from the demolition work they did, and also from the salvage of building materials, it was a very lucrative business. Like they did at this auction in Leicester.

105

Some of the chimneys they demolished weighed up to, and over a thousand tonnes and would have hundreds of thousands of bricks. Those that were in good condition would be cleaned up and resold to build new chimneys, houses or factories in the local areas.

Ive done a fair bit of demolition work myself down on the ground, its back breaking work. I`ve had my fair share of accidents at work as well. I broke my knee cap on one job in Stratford on Avon, shattered it would be a better description. It happened just a few weeks before Christmas. The multi millionaire gaffers actually offered to get me a "few beers" as compensation.

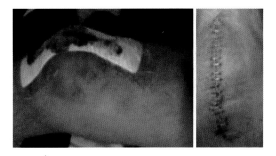

A few beers ! It was nearly two years before I could walk properly. They couldn`t care less, they even refused to call me an ambulance. They insisted they drove me home, because they must have seen it as some kind of an admission of liability. I heard afterwards they were telling people the injury couldn't be that bad as I didn't want an ambulance. I never heard from them from that day on, not to see how i was or anything. They were the same sort of greedy bastards as my old gaffers were.

You ache from head to toe, doing demolition work, your hands are covered in blisters and cuts. Your clothes, hair, and nose are thick with dust, you are coughing it up from your lungs for days afterwards if you don't wear a mask. You certainly earn your money in that job, and you sleep very well. Some of those chimney walls were up to 7 or 8 feet thick at the base, an extremely hard job knocking them down by hand with no power tools. I can't imagine doing that work all the way up there in the high winds, with a 200 or 300+ foot drop either side of you. Just climbing the ladders would be a good workout in itself for most people, let alone do a days work swinging pick axes once you'd reached the top.

Some of the family had terrible tempers when anyone upset them, great granddad in particular was a very hard, mean extremely volatile man when he wanted to be by all accounts. They enjoyed a good scrap because they were good at it. Im not trying to say they were supermen or anything, but the work hardened them.

A steeplejack is the best living example of a strong, silent man. He is usually physically powerful.

Steeplejacks were generally physically strong but very agile from clambering up and down ladders all day. They had very good balance that came from standing on narrow ledges in the wind, good reflexes from having to snatch at ropes or ladders when the wind caught them by surprise. They spent their days hitting walls with sledge hammers. Most of them had big, hard hands. If you wanted a job that could maybe give you an edge in a fight, you could do a lot worse than be a steeplejack. Just like a blacksmith was usually the strongest man in the village, steeplejacks were usually the rowdiest and up for a fight. They had a different outlook on life facing dangers that could kill them every day. They fought for fun in the old boxing booths, when they worked away up and down the country. After get hit by lumps of mortar and brick ends while they worked, getting hit by a bloke with gloves on would be nothing.

Great granddad was a broad barrel chested man, an unbeaten bare knuckle fighter so the stories go. He could punch his full weight of 16 stone with either hand very fast. One story was that he had a bare knuckle fight near where Redhill round - about is today near Birstall, on the edge of Belgrave. The fight supposedly lasted for 3 days, which I doubt, a lot of stories were exaggerated over time. It was for a giant cod, which he won.

The family were a rough lot, notoriously well known locally for drinking and fighting, but they were never bullies. A few of them in the modern family went on to be doormen or bouncers. Now the family aren't steeplejacking anymore they`re doing all sorts of jobs down on the ground.

There were some pretty hot tempered fiery characters in the family, according to most people iv spoken to in the family and people that knew them in the area. It was best not to upset them, not if you knew what was good for you, was the bottom line from most of the people i spoke to. One person on the Bygone Belgrave facebook group told me that one of them, one of dads cousins, its not fair for me to mention names out of respect for his family today, he could hit people very hard, one punch was enough. No one could touch him in his day he said.

When dad was 14 he was stood outside a shop on Harrison road, talking to two young girls about his own age, trying his best chat up lines out on them, when a lad of 18 came along bouncing a football. Dad was a skinny bloke with glasses, and the older lad started taking the piss out of him, trying to impress the girls. He threw the ball at dad. He asked him not to, but he threw it at him again. Dad told him again to pack it in, but he took no notice. He didn't like football or footballers at the best of times, so he wasn't going to stand for one taking the piss out of him like that. After the third time of throwing the ball at dad, he hit him once, and he bounced off the wooden post holding up the shop front and fell flat on his face. Dad said the front of the shop shook, and the wire rack holding the newspapers by the shop doorway fell off the wall. He never had to hit a man twice in his whole life he told me.

They were a very tight, close family, they had to be, their lives depended on each other every day. They had their fall outs and quite often it ended up getting physical, like it did with most families back then. I`ve spoken to people about the family in some of the pubs in Belgrave, 25 years ago or more. The Bulls head, the Hotel Belgrave, Talbot, Jungle, Balmoral, Liberal club the British legion. Pubs they used to drink in years and years ago. Some of the older people still remembered them. One bloke told me about one of the family, again im not mentioning names, it was one of granddads brothers. He

Eight or nine pints, and then doing that job. Unbelievable ! Another couple of drunk and disorderly`s up court in the next newspaper report.

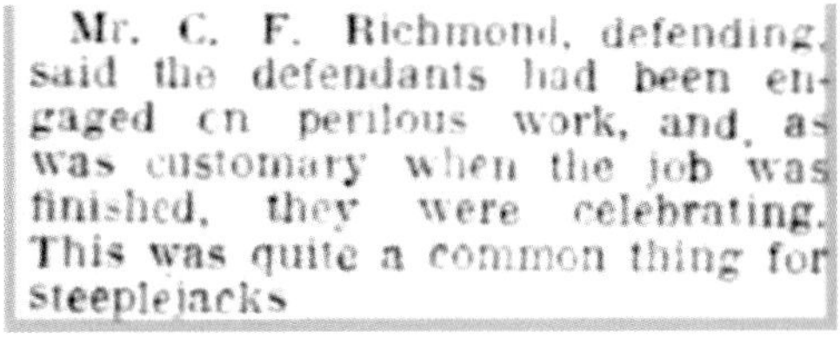

Mr. C. F. Richmond, defending, said the defendants had been engaged on perilous work, and, as was customary when the job was finished, they were celebrating. This was quite a common thing for steeplejacks

Mr. C. F. Richmond,

defending, said the defendants had been engaged on perilous work, and, as was customary when the job was finished, they were celebrating. This was quite a common thing for Steeplejacks.

****

Men drank before chimney death fall

Woman's body found on abbey roof

Men drank before chimney death fall

Two experienced steeplejacks had been drinking before they fell to their deaths from a tall chimney stack, a Birmingham inquest jury was told yesterday.

The jury returned a verdict of death by misadventure on James Edward Vaughan, aged' 25, of Bankside, Durham Estate, Hamstead, Birmingham , and William Ernest Tennant, aged 39, of Brandon Road, Hurst Green,

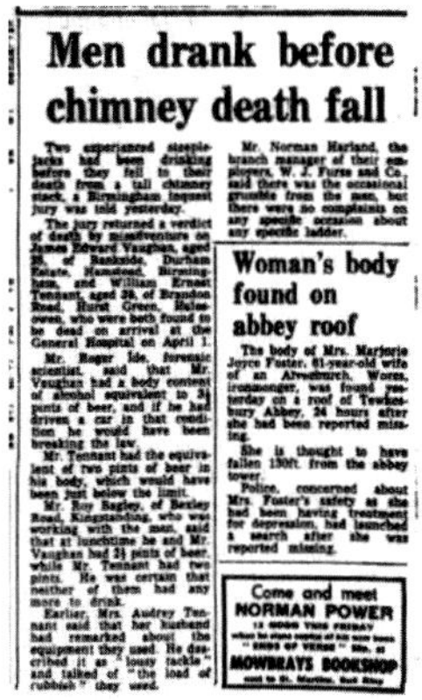

Halesowen, who were both found to be dead on arrival at the General Hospital on April 1. Mr. Roger fde, forensic scientist, said that Mr. Vaughan had a body content of alcohol equivalent to 3 pints of beer, and if he had driven a car in that condition he would have been breaking the law.

Mr. Tennant had the equivalent of two pints of beer in his body, which would have been just below the limit.

Mr. Roy Bagley, of Bexley Road, Kingstanding, who was working with the men, said that at lunchtime he and Mr. Vaughan had 2+ pints of beer. while Mr. Tennant had two pints. He was certain that neither of them had any more to drink.

Earlier, Mrs. Tennant said, That her husband had remarked about the equipment they used, he described it as "lousy tackle" and talked of, the load of rubbish they used.

Mr. Norman Harland, the branch manager of their em, ployers, W. J. Furze and Co.. said there was the occasional grumble from the men, but there were no complaints on any specific occasion about any specific ladder.

✱✱✱✱✱✱✱✱✱✱✱✱✱✱✱✱✱

The family enjoyed a good drink , but the family chose never to when they worked. It was their golden rule. Too many men were killed because of it. Not that Fred Dibnah ever needed a drink before he climbed, but when he said on tv he often had 5 pints at dinner and went back to work on a chimney, both dad and granddad thought it was irresponsible, it could get lesser steeplejacks killed listening to that. Respectfully I have to agree. I thought he was a great bloke, it fascinated me watching him work. His engineering mind enabled him to make the job easier. As far as steeplejacks go, he certainly brought something extra to the job. Watching him on the telly was the closest i could get to seeing the sort of work the family did.

Danger wise you could probably liken the work of a steeplejack to those who built the sky scrapers in America in the early 20th century. With a couple of differences. While they worked at greater heights, they didn`t have the worry the whole thing could collapse beneath them, because it was broken right through the middle half way up. Neither did the sky scraper men have to cope with the heat or fumes from the chimneys. The heat would scorch their clothes, the toxic fumes burnt their lungs and stung their eyes.

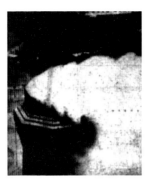

Most of the family had great sense of humours. They needed it to cope with all the crap they went through both at work and in their personal lives. Coming from a family of steeplejacks, they had more than their share of ups and downs, pardon the pun. Dad used to joke the toxic chimney fumes probably sent some of them a bit wappy, a bit nuts. Himself included probably.

A relative sent me this photo below, taken outside their terraced houses on Payne street. These in the next photo were either very ugly women, or they were up for a laugh.

Granddads brothers outside their house on Payne Street, no idea what year.

The family enjoyed a few pints but only ever after their work was done. All except one who was a teetotaller. They were a rum lot, notoriously rough. Well known locally for getting into trouble, so im told by quite a few in the family, and old Belgrave people who remembered them.

The old Belgrave working mens club had a long bar that was curved at one end. Years ago it was apparently known as Akiens corner, because there was usually one or more of them there having a few pints.

They never received any medals for the many acts of extreme bravery they did. I'm sure given the choice a fair few people would have sooner taken their chances going off to war, than do what they did. No disrespect intended when i say that. There were instances of people who got medals for rescuing steeplejacks who had been overcome by fumes at the tops of chimneys. They go up there once and get a medal for it. One steeplejack received the British empire medal for removing a policemans helmet from the top of the houses of parliament. A famous politician of that time recognised how important and daring their work was, likening their bravery to soldiers going off to war.

The family never got the chance very often to earn any medals. When they did go off to war they were brought back when it was discovered what work they did, they had reserved occupations. There were accounts of people claiming to be steeplejacks, just to avoid getting called up. To counter this cowardly trend steeplejacks were graded on the level of their experience. Years of experience would give a grade 1 level, exempting them from call up.

When they did go off to wars they saw some terrible things. Great grt uncle
Harold went off to fight in the Boer war in 1901. He wrote this letter home
and it was sent it in to a local Leicester paper, they published it in 1901.

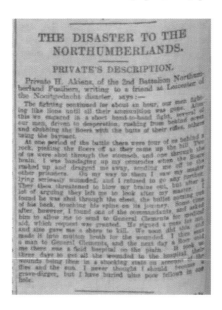

THE DISASTER TO THE NORTHUMBERLANDS.

PRIVATES DESCRIPTION.

Private Harold Akiens of the 2nd Battallion Northumberlands fusiliers, writing
to a friend at Leicester of the Nooitgedacht disaster, says :-

"The fighting continued for about an hour, our men were fighting like lions
until all their ammunition was gone. After this we engaged in a short hand to
hand fight, several of our men, driven to desperation, rushing from behind and
clubbing the boers with the butts of their rifles, others using the bayonet.

At one period of the battle there were four of us behind a rock, picking the Boers off as they came up the hill. Two of us were shot through the stomach, and one through the brain. I was bandaging up my comrades when the Boers rushed up and dragged me away, sending me off to the other prisoners. On my way to them i saw my master lying seriously wounded, and i refused to go any further.

They then threatened to blow my brains out, but after a lot of arguing they left me to look after my master. I found he was shot through the chest, the bullet coming out of his back, touching his spine on its journey. Sometime after however, i found one of the commandants and asked him to allow me to send to general Clements for medical aid. Which request was granted. He signed a pass for me and also gave me a sheep to kill. We soon did this. And made it into mutton. Broth for the wounded.

I then sent a man to General Clements and the next day a Boer told me there was a field hospital on the plain. It took us 3 days to get all the wounded to the hospital their wounds being then in a shocking state on account of the flies and the sun. I never thought i should become a grave digger, but i have buried nine poor fellows in one hole."

****

A lot of steeplejack firms were made up of generations of a family that climbed from a young age. They were born into the job just like my family were. Many of these climbing families only gave the job up, after they had a faller. It was too harrowing for them, seeing their loved one smashed to a pulp beyond recognition at the bottom of a chimney or a church steeple.

Usually within a year or two they would lose heart and find some other safer occupation. My great uncle Jesse was the only recorded one in the family to tragically fall to his death in 1913, in almost 300 years of climbing. He died just three days before his 18th birthday. He never even got to have his first pint. He was very sadly missed by the whole family, and his parents were buried with him at Welford cemetery.

They never gave up the work though inspite of Jesse falling, they carried on doing what they`d been doing for centuries. For a family to last as long as they did doing this brutally punishing, dangerous work, it was remarkable. I would doubt there being many families, if any, that stuck the job out for as long as they did. Pride in what they did kept them going. They used to say they were the oldest climbing family in England. They were probably right about that.

Jesse Akiens, aged 17, one of a famous family of steeplejacks, died in Leicester Royal Infirmary as a result of a fall from a high factory chimney in the town.

A lot of these articles appeared in newspapers all over the country. London, Birmingham, Manchester, Southampton, Glasgow, Belfast, all over the place. Internationally the family were written about in Canada, America and Australia to name a few.

The next newspaper article tells of when Great uncle Jesse fell from a chimney in Grandby street in the town in Leicester. The accident happened on a Saturday but he didn`t die until four days later on the Wednesday. He was just a young lad, killed doing his job.

LEICESTER STEEPLEJACK`S DEATH :

FOLLOWS FALL FROM A LADDER.

At the Leicester Infirmary, on Wednesday, Jesse Akiens (17), steeplejack, son of John Thomas Akiens, 33 Victoria road North, also a steeplejack, died as the result of injuries received from a fall on Saturday.

Deceased, who was in the employ of his father, was on Saturday afternoon employed with other workmen in repairing a chimney at Messrs. Moore, Eady and Murcott Goode`s works in Granby street. He went down to get some bolts. Soon afterwards a thud was heard and Akiens was found lying injured at the foot of the ladder. No one saw him fall, but a telephone wire some 20ft high was broken, showing he must have fallen from a higher point than that. He was taken to the Infirmary, but was so badly injured that from the first very little hopes were entertained of his recovery.

The Borough Coroner Mr. E. G. B. Fowler, conducted the inquest on Thursday, at the Infirmary. Mr J. E. Appleyard (Birmingham) H. M Inspector of factories was present.

Dr. Wilkinson said the deceased was admitted to the Infirmary suffering from injuries caused by a bad fall. There were cuts on the body, and the ribs on the right side were broken. There was a large wound in the right lung, and the deceased died from that injury.

Mrs. Ellen Akiens, the mother of deceased and the wife of a steeplejack, said her son was working in Granby street repairing a chimney shaft at Messrs. Moore, Eady and Murcott Goode`s factory. He told her after the accident that he went for some bolts and slipped and fell.

Albert Lees a steeplejack, of the same address, said he was in the employ of John Thomas Akiens, and the deceased worked with him. The shaft was about 80 feet high, ladders being up one side. There was a chain across the top with dogs into the sides, the scaffold being fixed to them. The chimney came through a glass roof. On Saturday they had finished the job except for two bolts, and the deceased went down the ladders to get them.

Soon after he saw the rope running very fast through the pulley, and he judged that the deceased felt himself slip, and tried to save himself by taking hold of the rope.

If he had caught hold of both ropes he would have saved himself. Witness heard a thud and ran down and found him on the glass roof. The two bolts were found in deceased`s pockets, so he was coming up the ladder when he slipped. He must have fallen across a telephone wire, for one was broken.

By Mr. Appleyard Witness did not know that the deceased was carrying anything except the bolts. When deceased fell none of the ladders came away. After the accident they were all in position. A verdict of accidental death was returned.

****

During the first world war they kept the Leicester hospital chimneys in good working order. I haven`t found any other newspaper stories of what else they did during the war years yet, other than they demolished buildings and chimneys damaged in the Zeppelin raids.

During the second world war they camouflaged power stations, munitions factories, military installations, painted radio towers, things they couldn't talk about at the time. Those stories were never in the papers, well they wouldn't be, would they. The family were written about in the papers over many years, but nothing at all about any of them during both of the war years. So what were they doing exactly, id love to find out if anyone knows.

The next articles show the sort of work steeplejacks did during the second world war. The family worked on these cooling towers in Leicester camouflaging them by painting trees on them. He visited Germany after the war and they were very keen for him to work on the bomb damaged cities. He was offered lots of money and was very tempted, but he decided not to, England needed the kind of work people like him could do. I think he`d spent enough time away from his family during the war. He worked in Coventry for a while after the Germans bombed it.

The cooling towers below in Leicester the family worked on.

CAMOUFLAGE... Leicester Electricity Generating Station is having its cooling towers camouflaged. Steeplejacks are painting trees and foliage over the masonry, with results that should disguise the station at the county cricket ground.

✱✱✱✱✱✱✱✱✱✱✱✱✱✱✱✱

Cooling towers in Leicester
were the first in the world to be
camouflaged at the beginning of
the last war, said Mr. Akiens.
And it was his firm which carried out the work. They painted
on pictures of houses and trees.

"The only thing we could not
camouflage was the tower
shadow," said Mr. Akiens.

The work they did at Leicester's electricity plant. was followed by similar work in many
other cities throughout the country.

Cooling towers in Leicester were the first in the world to be camouflaged at the beginning of the last war, said Mr Akiens. And it was his firm which carried out the work. They painted on pictures of houses and trees. The only thing we couldn't camouflage was the shadow of the tower. The work they did at Leicester`s Electricity plant was followed by similar work in many other cities throughout the country

****

Iv got all my granddad and dads business records going back to 1946. Every chimney, factory and steeple he worked on, every demolition, pointing and painting job. I`ve got all the records even down to just about every nail he bought. Everything that went through the books. He earned a fair bit of money after the war through to the mid 60`s. Then times got very tough. Most of the chimneys and buildings he worked on have gone now. But there are no records at all of what he did before 1946, nothing about what he did during the war. There could be some truth to some of the other wartime stories he told. These are the earliest entries in granddads business book after the war.

Steeplejacks were allowed extra and sometimes unlimited petrol rations during the war so they could carry out their important work. This bloke below got caught fiddling his rations and ended up in court.

> Petroleum Office said petrol coupons for the car were issued in connection with the younger defendant's business as a steeplejack and were confined to "going from one job to another with trailer inspecting mill chimneys, church steeples, etc." Mr. Kilner submitted

The Petroleum office said petrol coupons for the car were issued in connection with the younger defendants business as a steeplejack and were confined to going from one job to another with trailer inspecting mill chimneys, church steeples, etc. Mr Kilner submitted there was no case against Herbert brooks as the evidence had shown.

****

Granddad was also allowed unlimited petrol coupons during the war because of all his invaluable work, demolishing or repairing the chimneys of the factories that got bombed or the steeples of churches. He told me he sold a fair bit of it to family, friends, neighbours and business associates, so they could go about their business. He did very well out of it apparently. No one told him he couldn't sell it. If they did, he probably didn't hear them.

This is one of the families climbing belts, this one was my Dads.

Now on display for the Leicester City Museum and Arts Department, as part of an industrial heritage of Leicester theme they`re doing.

Some of the other tools they used. Different hammers and chisels for different jobs. The ropes were thick, very rough on your hands, and a bit smelly to be honest. It would be very easy to get rope burns off one of them. Every morning they had to be checked for the slightest signs of cuts or fraying. If any were found the ropes would be burnt immediately.

They were supposed to use these belts when they were riding the seat, the bosuns chair, or to hook on the ladders to give them a breather. They only used them on the ladders to stretch out when they were painting or pointing the chimney. Whenever dad was at the top of a chimney or a steeple he would have a good look round at what was below them. As unbelievable as this sounds, they didn't wear them very often because of one unique climbing philosophy. The belts were mainly worn by the children and those with less climbing experience. I don`t know if any others in the family thought this way but dad and granddad certainly did. The belts tied them to the chimney. If the pulley failed or if anything happened to the rope, they risked hanging themselves or falling tied up in the ropes, to their deaths on the boiler house roofs below.

Without the belt, they could instinctively kick out off the wall, in the hope of aiming themselves for the softest landing available. A river, a tree, a bush, anything but solid ground, piles of broken bricks or the boiler house roofs. They were ready to turn a fall, into a dive. Dad told me they had nothing to lose if it ever happened, it was shit or bust. I know how mad that sounds, but they were a pretty mad lot. That philosophy possibly saved Granddads life a few times when he fell.

Back in the old days before my dads generation, when the kids stepped out of line, they didn`t get hit with dads ordinary belt buckle like so many kids did back then. In our family, they got belted with one of those climbing belts. A terrifying thought for anyone getting beaten with that scary looking heavy iron hook. They were probably more afraid of these belts than anything they ever had to climb. It was probably the only thing some of them were afraid of, they didn`t seem to give a shit about anything else. Great granddad loved his family and had a very fierce sense of loyalty to them, he was a harsh, strict, but fair man. He had some pretty brutal ways of keeping them all in check. It was how he was bought up, like his dad was bought up, they had a very tough upbringing.

There will be others in the family that have grown up with these stories, or versions of them, but these are what I was told. I`m not saying they were true, I wasn't there I didn't see any of them myself obviously. What i`m saying is, it`s true that i was told them. There will be stories in this they haven`t heard before and i`m sure they will undoubtedly have stories about what their branches of the family got up to, that i haven`t heard before.

SATURDAY, 24th JULY, 1937   THE ILLUSTRATED LEICESTER CHRONICLE 9

OTHER PEOPLE'S JOBS—NO. 3

THRILLS IN THE WORK OF THE STEEPLEJACK

Miraculous Escapes Of A Leicester Championship Family

GIRL WHO FIXED WEATHER-COCK ON ST. MARK'S STEEPLE

They were the sort of people who would stand up in a crowded bar and tell people to mind their language in front of their wives. It was ok for them to swear in front of their wives when they were pissed off, but they didn't like anyone else doing it. My dad used to, so did granddad, he didn`t like anyone swearing in front of any women. Great granddad certainly told people, quite a few times in some of the old Belgrave pubs. I never bothered, my ex-missus swore more than most blokes.

There were a few incidents that ended very badly for some men, because they would not take the warning from him. Something pretty bad happened in a pub called the Fosse Tavern, that was another story both dad and granddad told me. One man in another pub was hit so hard, he bled from his mouth, his nose, both eyes and both ears, from a single punch. He never regained consciousness and died several days later from his injuries, so the story went. Dad, granddad and a few others in the family have also told the same stories about some of what happened. I`ve no reason to doubt them, even though he never made the papers for them. I did find this next article though. The man had very similar injuries to the one in the story we were told, and he was a steeplejack. He could have been a rival, they could have worked together, they could have fell out over work or money. The article could be related to that story, or it could have had absolutely sod all to do with it, but it sounds plausible to me the two could be related.

125

About four o'clock on Thursday afternoon a man was found lying on the pavement in Belgrave gate badly injured. His name proved to be WM. Tamidge, following the occupation of a steeplejack and living in Southampton street. He was discovered outside the crown and cushion public house insensible, with blood flowing from both eyes and ears and with evident signs of serious injury. When P.C Smart arrived upon the scene, a large crowd had collected, and Dr Chapman, of Belgrave gate, had been summoned, and was rendering what assistance he could to the injured man. The horse ambulance-wagon was fetched from the fire station, in Rutland street, and the man was conveyed as speedily as circumstances would permit to the Infirmary. He was still unconscious when he arrived there, and was evidently suffering from severe injuries to the skull.

****

There was one story a few of us were told, about when the family were working down in London. A big burly beefeater decided to give one of the younger Akiens a slap, I don't know why. He was probably being cocky, over boisterious, or possibly drunk. Someone told great granddad about it. He went and found that beefeater. Their left hands were tied together and off they went. I doubt the beefeater had much say in the matter. If what happened to him was true, it was shockingly brutal. The beef eater come the end of it, had a face like a plate of raw liver they said. That sort of violence was commonplace back then, that`s how they sorted things out.

126

Granddad told me once, a plain clothes policeman knocked the door of their house on Payne street. He had come to chastise granddad for scrumping in the gardens of the big houses on Loughborough road. He only got a few words out before great granddad knocked him out with one punch on the doorstep. He didn`t know he was a copper. He never got done for it and it wasn`t in the papers, not that I could find anyway, because he was such a prominent freemason, so granddad said, who knows.

Granddad was the youngest of 15 children. He remembered when he was a young lad, they had a long dining table where they all sat down to have meals at. Like the waltons he used to joke, but they were steeplejacks, not lumberjacks. None of them ever left the house for work in a morning with a dirty neck, if ever they did they were made to go back inside and wash again. He remembered when he was about 5 or 6, his mam asking him to do something for her. All he said was, " ok mam, i`ll do it in a minute." He told me he woke up at teatime with a pounding headache. Great granddad punched him. He would not take disrespect off anyone and nor would you disrespect his wife, whoever you were. Thank fully granddad wasn`t like that with my dad or any of his siblings.

There were hundreds if not thousands of steeplejacks who lost their lives for all manner of reasons. Rotting brickwork crumbling beneath them, unsecure ladders, ropes snapping, or getting burnt through from the heat of the chimney, chimneys collapsing, falling masonry, pulleys failing, lumps of mortar hitting and knocking them off balance during demolition, being overcome by fumes, scaffolding collapsing, or an invisible gust of wind throwing them off.

There were cases of steeplejacks being struck by lightning as they swung their pickaxes. Probably for the same reasons an average 27 people get killed every year playing golf. Sometimes they were killed because they`d been drinking. In some cases a whole gang of steeplejacks were killed at once when chimneys collapsed. These newspapers below are just a handful from thousands of newspaper articles written about them.

PLAYING WITH DEATH FOR A LIVING.

Glamour of national service surrounds the proffered self-sacrifice of the submarine crew. The "steeple jack" follows his risky trade because he needs the money he earns in that way, remarks a contributor to the current issue of "T.A.T. (Tales and Talk). Not long since a man was seen working on the outside of the sloping dome of St. Paul's Cathedral. Spectators turned away with shudders, and declared it foolhardy that anyone should risk his life in such manner, as hazardous those who may be truly ranked as "men unafraid."

PLAYING WITH DEATH FOR A LIVING

Glamour of national service surrounds the proffered self-sacrifice of the submarine crew. The "steeplejack" follows his risky trade because he needs the money he earns in that way, remarks a contributor to the current issue of T.A.T (Tales and talk.) Not long since a man was seen working on the outside of the sloping dome of St Pauls Cathederal. Spectators turned away with shudders, and declared it foolhardy that anyone should risk his life in such a manner as hazardous those who may be truly ranked "men unafraid."

****

In some of the articles they printed the injuries they suffered were truly shocking. They knew what was likely to happen to them if they ever fell. Their mangled, mutilated bodies were sometimes unrecognisable. In many cases nearly every bone in their bodies were broken. They were very brave people, in my opinion they were unsung heroes. The work they did wasn`t quite as dangerous as fighter pilots during the war, but it wasn`t far off.

Below are just some of the newspaper reports of terrible accidents.

128

STEEPLEJACK TRAGEDY

TWO MEN FALL 120 FEET

Two steeplejacks met with a terrible death on Saturday morning, falling from a chimney 120 feet high. Their bodies alighted on a large quantity of broken bricks and were almost beyond recognition.

＊＊＊＊＊＊＊＊＊＊＊＊＊＊＊＊

SHOCKING DEATH OF A STEEPLEJACK

As a steeplejack named Henry Gilbert was engaged doing some work at the weathercock on top of the St. Matthews Church spire, Sheffield on Wednesday, the vane to which he was fastened broke away, and he fell headlong into the street a distance of 125 feet. His head was fearfully injured, and some of his brains were scattered several feet from where he fell, death of course being instantaneous.

＊＊＊＊＊＊＊＊＊＊＊＊＊＊＊＊

STEEPLEJACK DASHED TO PIECES

William Mason, an Oldham steeplejack, employed in repairing a chimney at the Rainey works, Bents lane, Bredbury, met with a shocking death last Friday. Mason, who worked for Messr`s Jos, Ball and Co, was being hoisted up the chimney to the top of the chimney by a rope. When within a couple of yards from the top, the rope broke and the man fell to the ground a distance of 100 feet. He was dashed almost to pieces, before the eyes of his mates and a crowd of spectators.

****

FEARFUL DEATH A STEEPLE-JACK.

130

On Monday afternoon William Dunbar aged 26, belonging to Dundee, met with fearful death at Iaverness. .He was engaged repairing the steeple of the Free High Church in the town. When, either through the coldness of the weather or through becoming giddy, he lost his hold and fell from a height of about 70 feet. He allighted on an iron railing, on which he was impaled. His death was instantaneous. Another Steeple-Jack engaged higher up than Dunbar was terribly shocked by the sight. Dunbar was native of Loudon.

****

Quite often when they did fall, there would be large crowds of people there to see it happen. They nearly always drew large crowds to watch them work.

The wooden staging was later replaced by scaffolding. These photos above are some of the wider family at work, Dads cousins and uncles. The photo on the right was published in the Leicester Mercury after a relative sent it in.

131

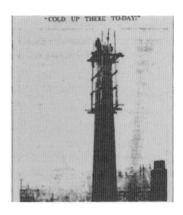

The chimneys they worked on where the boilers weren`t still lit, were sometimes frozen solid from the rain and freezing cold winds.

This chimney was demolished by the family in the 1960`s in St Matthews in Leicester when it was first built. The bloke standing next to it in the photo when it fell looked pretty relaxed about what was going on just a few feet away. It was one of dads cousins, but im not sure which.

The lower classes to many of the Victorians didn`t matter, some of them would fight tooth and nail to get out of paying people what they`d earnt. The judge in the case below surprisingly ruled in favour of the steeplejack, not the greedy tight fisted factory owner. I know the feeling very well.

STEEPLEJACKS WAGES

7s 6d an Hour.

I Judge Bacon was enlightened at the Blooms. bury County Court on Wednesday on matters connected with steeplejacks, especially with reference to their emoluments, calculated to raise a spirit of envy amongst men who follow other callings not so remunerative. The plaintiff was a man evidently of no little importance in tbe steeplejack world. He sued for £ 3 15s, being 15 hours' work at 58 per hour, The work In question consisted of bricking up a defective chimney, and the services of a climbing man or steeplejack were necessitated. The defendants contested the claim on excessive. The "steeplejack" was called, and stated that he generally received 7a 6d per hour, and sometimes more. There were very few men now who could climb a chimney. On behalf of the defendants, Messrs Watson and Company, it was contended that the work was such as might have been performed by a chimney sweep in a few minutes. The judge evidently considered that the steeplejack was worthy of his hire at the rate stipulated, for he gave the plaintiff the verdict, with costs.

* * * * * * * * * * * * * * * * *

This next bit is about my own experience working in a factory, iv only added it because its quite relevant, its nothing personal. If it was id be writing a lot more than just two pages worth. All im doing is writing about my time there. Im not writing anything I cant prove in court, if it should ever come to that. I started work there from leaving school at 16. There were a great bunch of lads to work with, they gave me the nickname the Young Un. When I was valued and needed, I enjoyed working there, learning all the trades they needed me to.

I can fully understand why the family chose to work above these places instead of in them, if they were anything like this place. The health and safety was abysmal. I worked my fingers to the bone almost for the gaffer. Blood would literally seep through the skin on my fingers because of the sort of work I did for them. When I got home from work at night it felt as though my hands had been dipped in acid. Ironically, I didn't fall from a stack like some of the family did in the past, a stack fell on me, a stack of furniture 20ft high. It was like an avalanche of furniture falling on me. I could have claimed against them but I didn't, they would have been closed down by the health and safety if I made the legitimate claim, and all my workmates would have all been out of work, so the gaffer told me. I didnt want compensation for the injuries, just loss of earnings for the time I had to take off. I ended up being bullied into accepting less than a third of what I would have earnt. They packed furniture right up to the rafters, as much as they could cram in wherever they could. The black hole in the 1st picture behind the ladders, we had to carry 3 seater settees and wardrobes through that. They even built shelves for stock above our heads where we worked. They didn't listen to any of the lads complaints. It was their factory, "They could do whatever the hell they liked", we were told.

Some things don't change, they weren`t that much different to the greedy Victorian factory owners really. Similarly to the steeplejacks, when you`re a vital part of the factory operations, loyally working all the hours they needed, for a lot of years like I did, they think the world of you, they can`t` do enough for you. Like lending you money if you needed it, adding interest of course.

But when you`re not needed anymore, they couldn't give a shit. I could kind of accept that, its progress. It was the underhanded way they went about it that I found difficult to take, my job was shipped overseas bit by bit. They imported the furniture from the far east that we used to make. Sooner than pay me the redundancy I deserved after all those years, they just kept cutting my hours. No way would they pay me nearly 18 years of redundancy money, not if they could force me out for free. Had they done the decent, right thing and paid me what was due, you would be reading a completely different positive chapter about my time working there. Inspite of working for them for all those years, when it came to it, I was just a council estate scumbag after their money. In the end I had no choice but to leave, I couldn't afford to work there. Some weeks I was paid a lot less than the legal minimum amount, required to live on, if you were on the sick ! (£52.20 at the time) and they were happy to pay me that pittance, however illegal it was. Everyone had a pay rise one year except me. I didn't find out for months. The gaffer backdated it but refused point blank to backdate the overtime. I did 55-65 hours most weeks so he saved himself a few quid with that trick. I met some great lads there and we had some brilliant laughs over the years. It was a shame it ended so very very badly, when it hadn't needed to. It was no way to treat a young un.

When granddad was 15 he was involved in a motorbike accident near Melton Mowbray. His rubber suit caught fire and he was engulfed in flames. He was very badly burned all over, bedridden covered in bandages and ointments for a whole year. When Granddad was in hospital, the doctors asked grt granddads permission to have granddads legs amputated. He asked if that would guarantee he lived, they said no they couldn`t guarantee it. So he told them no.

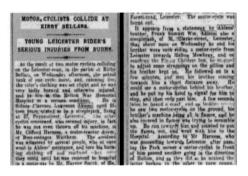

MOTOR CYCLISTS COLLIDE AT KIRBY BELLARS.

YOUNG LEICESTER RIDER`S SERIOUS INUJURIES FROM BURNS.

As the result of two motor cyclists colliding on the Leicester road, in the Parish of Kirby Bellars, on Wednesday afternoon, the petrol tank of one cyclist burst, and catching fire, the riders clothing was set alight and he was very badly burned and otherwise injured, and he lies in the Melton War Memorial Hospital in a serious condition.

He is Sidney Clarence Laurence Akiens, aged fifteen years, stated to be a steeplejack, living at 27 Payne street Leicester. The other cyclist concerned , who escaped injury, in fact he was not even thrown off his machine, is Mr. Clifford Harness, a motor tractor driver of Rose Cottages Waltham.

The accident was witnessed by several people, who at once went to Akiens assistance, and tore his burning clothing off and rendered what help they could until he was removed to hospital in a motor car by Mr. Harrow Smith, of 25a Forest road Leicester. The motor cycle was burnt out.

It appears from a statement by Akiens brother Frank Samuel Akiens, also a steeplejack, of 32 Clarke street, Leicester, that about noon on Wednesday he and his brother were each riding a motor cycle towards Melton Mowbray, and on reaching the Flying Childers Inn, he stopped to adjust some strappings on the pillion and his brother kept on. He followed on in a few minutes and met his brother coming towards him a short distance away. He could see a motor cyclist behind his brother, and he put his hand to signal for him to stop, and then rode past him.

A few seconds later he heard a crash and on looking round he saw two motor cycles on the ground, his brothers machine being all in flames was trying to scramble up. He ran towards him and assisted to put the flames out, and went with him to hospital. According to Mr. Harness, who was proceeding towards Leicester after passing the Park corner a motorcyclist in front of him passed another going in the direction of Melton, and as they did so he noticed the latter beckon to the other to turn round.

He was about four yards behind the cyclist in front, who suddenly turned to the right across the road, and the front wheel of Mr. Harness machine hit the centre of the other one, which was being ridden by young Akiens, knocking him, and his motor cycle immediately burst into flames and set his clothing on fire. He ran down the side of the road towards Kirby Bellars and then collapsed. He retained consciousness, although having such serious injuries, including his hair and eyebrows burnt off, and the thumb of his right hand. The condition of Akiens yesterday was unchanged.

****

Great granddad took a year off work to help nurse him back to full health. At a time before the nhs his various treatments were very costly, it nearly bankrupted the business. It cost a small fortune in those days for granddad just to have baths in pure olive oil. It was thought that would help heal the burns all over his body.

Before the accident they were quite well off, i have a copy of great granddads will. They owned quite a lot of land in Thurlaston, several plots a thousand yards long each. They owned properties in Leicester and St Helens where they were based in the north, so they could work on the many Lancashire mill chimneys up there. The women all wore fur coats and had fine jewellery.

When you consider they came from nothing in those poverty stricken times, they did very well. Their story could be described as one of rags to riches, and back again, sadly. They didn't make a ridiculous amount of money, but they did very well coming from nothing.

Granddad had the newest pioneering surgeries at the time. They put skin grafts on his nose using frog skin. He would later joke he worried he`d end up with a bright green nose. The thumb and two smaller fingers on his right hand were so badly burnt they had to be amputated. He only had the two victory fingers.

Today that injury might be considered a disability to a steeplejack. Im sure it would`ve ended the working life of most of them. The steeplejacks had hard lives anyway, but granddads must have been the hardest of any of them, having to climb with his hand how it was.

I remember in the pub he could only carry a pint glass by the bottom in his right hand. He could only use his left hand to use a lump hammer at work. Granddad never let it be a disability to him, he just got on with the job he was born to do. He had to pretty much learn to do everything left handed. He did all his own mechanics and he could write just as well with either hand.

While the Prince was inspecting the guard of honour of boy scouts, he recognised scout Sid Akiens and remembered an incident of last year when Akiens was injured, through his motorcycle catching fire at Kirby Bellars. The Prince was driving past when the accident happened, and stopped his car and asked if he could be of help. The Prince yesterday asked Akiens how he was getting on, and wished him good luck.

****

1929 at the Leicester agricultural show with the prince of Wales looking at granddads hand. The last time he saw him he was in flames on the roadside.

138

PRINCE AT LEICESTER

CHAT WITH INJURED BOY SCOUT.

The Prince of Wales visited the Leicestershire Agricultural Show to-day. Rain was falling, but thousands of people gathered in the streets to see the Prince drive in an open car to the show ground with the Lord Mayor (Ald. H. Hand).

On his arrival there he was greeted by Boy Scouts, and talked for some time to Scout Sid Akiens, who was injured last year when his motor-cycle caught fire at Kirby Bellars. The Prince was driving past in his car at the time, and offered to take Akiens to the nearest hospital.

The Prince now asked him how he was getting on. "I hope you have been able to get back to your work," he said. "Good luck! I hope you will get on all right."

CHAT WITH INJURED BOY SCOUT. : The Prince of Wales visited the Leicestershire agricultural show today. Rain was falling, but thousands of people gathered in the streets to see the Prince drive in an open car to the show ground with the lord mayor (Ald. H. Hand). On his arrival there he was greeted by boy scouts, and talked for some time to scout Sid Akiens, who was injured last year when his motor cycle caught fire at Kirby Bellars. The Prince was driving past in his car at the time, and offered to take Akiens to hospital. The Prince now asked him how he was getting on. " I hope you have been able to work," he said " Good Luck, i hope you will get on alright"

****

139

J. T. Akiens junior moved to Burton because of all the work there on the brewery chimneys. He was very well known in that area and was written about in the papers for some of his work quite a lot. Iv added a few of the ones I found.

Who is the speediest steeplejack ? A few months ago Mr. Aiken, of Burton, raced to the top of Messrs. Allsopp's chimney opposite the "Observer" Office in an incredibly short space of time. He said that he was about to fix his ladders, and when one of our staff went out about 15 minutes later the steeplejack was turning the corner of the upper projecting stonework. Leicester steeplejacks have now fixed ladders to a 100ft. chimney in 20 minutes 10 seconds, thereby it is claimed, setting up a record in ???????, but to the ordinary persons who spend most of his time with feet planted on mother earth of plaited on speed mother earth (or the substitute Madly provided by or private enterprise) This appears to be one of lifes endeavors in which the rule should be slow but sure

****

This article tells of a chimney the family felled, beside another firm dropping another chimney. They cocked it up and caused loads of damage, £1000 worth. You could buy four or five semi detached houses for that back then. It sounds like it was a spectacular cock up

GIANT CHIMNEY FALLS ON MALTINGS.

TWO BURTON STACKS FELLED IN ONE DAY.

A THOUSAND POUNDS OF DAMAGE.

The unique spectacle of the falling of two huge chimney stacks was witnessed by a number of Burtonians on Friday.

The first chimney, which measured 10 feet 2 inches across the square base, and about 5 feet across the top, and weighed 250 tons, was situated at Messrs. Bass and Co.'s Grange well pumping station, Grange Street.

The second was adjoining Horninglow Railway Station.

In its collapse, the second chimney caught the end of Messrs. Marston, Thompson and Evershed's No. 6 maltings, causing damage estimated by the firm at about £1,OOO.

The stack twisted in the act of falling, and broke in two. Had it twisted in the opposite direction, possibly houses in Derby Road would have been wrecked.

The steeplejack to whom tho work of felling Messrs. Bass's chimney was Mr. J. T. Akiens, of 1, Paget Street, Burton, whose father, grandfather and great-grandfather before him followed the most hazardous of calling of steeplejack.

The chimney, the walls of which were three feet thick at the base and had a heavy stone cap, was octagonal in shape. It had been built 43 years, and had to be removed because the pumping station has been electrified and the ground was required.

Mr. Akiens felled it by the improved method of which he was one of the first exponents. Instead of propping up the chimney as the brickwork at the base was cut away and then setting fire to the timber, the four men engaged, remarkable though it seems, entrust their lives to an ordinary penny cane. This is how it was done. Four men set to work making a hole 2 feet 3 inches high and two feet wide in the wall at the base; the cane, which was 3/8 inch thick, being vertically between the upper and lower edges the out. The object of the cane was to give the first indication that the huge mass was on the move. As a matter of fact the cane tell-tale always gives 3 minutes warning, and the men have ample time to get away. This was precisely 'what happened.

THE CRASH

The cane, which was naturally watched with increasing care, quivered as it began to take the weight, and then bowed perceptibly, the men hurriedly packed up and got clear. Shortly afterwards, the whole mass of masonry began to recline and then creaking in the centre, fell with a resounding roar, followed by a column of dust.

The steeplejack desired the chimney to fall in a line rather away from the parallel to the road, and to do this it was necessary to twist the chimney as it fell. Mr Akiens achieved his object by cutting out four inches beyond the point of equal balance on the one side and within twelve inches of the point of equal balance on the other.

The column spread itself out on the ground when it fell over a length of 100 feet, and then portions of the debris were thrown a few yards further. The old transformer house had been previously removed and the great stack thus fell clear of any buildings.

AVOIDS UNEQUAL BURNING OF TIMBER

The great advantage of the cane tell tale method, says Mr Akiens, is that it does away with the danger caused by inequal burning away of the timber props. As soon as the cane quivers a horizontal crack appears three courses below the top of the cut.

The steeplejack has to take into calculation, besides the height and weight of the chimney, the atmospheric pressure and the state of the wind, which must be on the leeward- so that his work waits for favourable weather conditions.

Among those who witnessed the fell were Colonel J Gretton, M.P Mr. Smith (Messrs Bass and Co.`s chief engineer, Mr. S H. Wormwell.

AN UNEXPECTED CRASH

CHIMNEY FALLS ON MALTINGS

The unexpected happened close by Horninglow Station, where a much larger chimney was being felled by another firm by the instructions of Messrs. Marstons.

The stack was within a few feet of the Malthouse, and some 30 yards or so from the nearest houses on Derby Road. The chimney was 16 feet wide at the bottom and six feet at the top, and the stone coping probably weighed about seven tons.

WITNESSED BY HUNDREDS

Situated as it was in so confined a space, it was necessary to calculate the fall to a nicety, but unfortunately, as stated, the column twisted in falling. Happily, it twisted towards the malting, from which the men had been evacuated, rather than the Derby Road, or the damage might have been much worse, and possibly, lives endangered.

However, the precaution had been taken by the inhabitants of leaving their houses just before the fall occurred. The collapse was witnessed by hundreds of people, and much excitement prevailed.

AN AWKWARD JOB

The work was undertaken by a local firm of contractors, whose foreman has had long experience as a steeplejack.

The manager of the firm stated on Saturday: "It was a very awkward job, in a confined space, and unfortunately , one of those accidents which sometimes happen, despite all precautions, occurred. We had not intended to drop the chimney until this morning, but it started cracking, and it was not considered safe to leave it up for the night.

The packing which had been placed in the hole cut in the wall at the base off the chimney was set on fire, and within about minutes the fall occurred. She started to fall beautifully, the column leaving the base, but as she rolled over the chimney twisted away in the direction of the malting and broke.

"I think about £200 or £300 will clear the damage. At six o`clock this morning we started a gang of men clearing away the site, and we are proceeding forthwith to repair the damage. We shall have it put right in a short time.

LIKE AN EARTHQUAKE TREMOR

The chimney was built about 1892 or 1893, and had not been used for years. Hence its removal was decided upon, especially as the bricks and stone were required for another purpose.

After the fall everything was obscured for a few minutes by a huge column of smoke and dust, but it had been seen that the stack was falling across the building. The roar could be heard from a great distance, and residents in Sydney Street said that they felt a distinct tremor, like an earthquake shock.

144

When the dust and smokescreen cleared it was seen that huge masses of bricks were piled up against the malting, and the roof and part of the walls had been smashed in.

Great steel girders in the roof were bent like tin. Indeed, the wreckage reminded one of the scene after a Zeppelin raid.

Fortunately, the boilers below were undamaged, and work in the malting will not be seriously interfered with. A quantity of masonry was flung into two gardens, some of the fencing was smashed. Loose bricks even found their way on to the railway siding on the other side of the malt house.

* * * * * * * * * * * * * * * *

BURTON STEEPLEJACK AT WORK ON DONINGTON CHURCH SPIRE.

Above we produce a photograph which shows Mr J. T. Akiens, a Burton Steeplejack, and his assistants, at work on the spire of Donnington church, which is to be partially pulled down and then reconstructed. Mr Akiens in on the left of the lower platform, and his son is on the top one.

* * * * * * * * * * * * * * * *

BURTON STEEPLEJACKS AT WORK

Our photograph shows steeplejacks in the employ of the Burton and Derbyshire Stonestill Co., of station street, Burton upon Trent, at work on the the chimney of a well known Burton firm. The company have expert men of many years experience in all kinds of steeplejack work, and the firm has a reputation of 200 years to place at the service of their clients. It is interesting to note that they have treated some of the most important buildings in Burton and Derbyshire.

＊＊＊＊＊＊＊＊＊＊＊＊＊＊＊

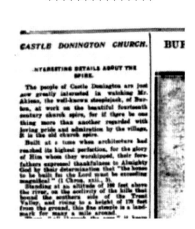

CASTLE DONNINGTON CHURCH. INTERESTING DETAILS ABOUT THE SPIRE.

The people of Castle Donnington are just now greatly interested in watching Mr. Akiens, the well known steeplejack of Burton at work on the beautiful fourteenth century church spire. For if there be one thing more than another rewarded with loving pride and admiration by the village, it is the old church spire.

Built at a time when architecture had reached its highest perfection, for the glory of him whom they worshipped, their fore fathers expressed thankfulness to Almighty God by their determination that "the house to be built for the Lord must be exceeding magnifical " (Chron. xxii.. 5).

Standing at an altitude of 100 feet above the river, on the acclivity of the hills that bound the southern side of the Trent Valley, and rises to a height of 170 feet from the ground, this fine steeple is a landmark for many a mile around.

There. "all through the ages," it keeps watch and ward over the little town at its feet, but having been assailed with unmitigated fury by the storms of 600 winters that gather strength in the valley below, some signs of the unequal contest are beginning to show themselves, and Messrs. Currey and Thompson , architects of great experience in church work, leave been called in to advise, and the work of repair has been entrusted to Mr. Akiens of Burton. Mr. Akiens and his men have repaired many well-known spires, including Queniborough, several in Leicester and Derby, and Sawley. In the very early years of the last century some 20 feet of the top of the Spire were rebuilt by Mr. George Garton, a fine old craftsman, and a native of the 'place. He lies buried under the shadow of the beautiful building he saved from destruction. But, unfortunately, his work was pulled about in 1888, and the spire made structurally defective. The work now in progress is designed to remedy this and to restore the spire to its appearance as the villagers remember it 40 years ago, before Its beauty was marred by ignorant tinkering, and what is still better, to its condition when it came fresh from the hands of its builders, about the year 1325.

Treasures of ancient art and craft must, be preserved at any cost, and handed down to our children unimpaired, and the people of Castle Donnington feel that they are doing nothing less than their bounden duty In using every endeavour to make the old church secure against the remotest chance of harm, so far as is humanly possible, not only because it is a priceless masterpiece of a bygone age, when men built for love, but also because of the precious memories that gather round an old building. " for. indeed," as Ruskin says. "the greatest glory of a building is not in its stones, nor in its gold. Its glory is in its age, and in that deep sense of voicefulness, of stern watching., of mysterious sympathy; any, even of approval or condemnation, which we have feel in walls that have been long washed by the passing wave of humanity"

****

GALE SNAPS TOWN HALL FLAGSTAFF

Alarming List Over King Edward Place

l BURTON STEEPLEJACKS' TICKLISIH TASK.

ALARM was caused in King Edward Place on Thursday night when the 40-feet flagstaff which crowns the Town Hall clock tower, leaned over at an angle of 45 degrees out of the perpendicular. Fears were entertained that with an increase in the force of the wind the pole would crash into the Square 120 feet below.

The discovery was made by Mr. C. J. Sherratt, the Town Hall keeper, and at once Messrs. J. T. Akiens, junior, of Moor Street, the well-known Burton firm of steeplejacks. were sent for. Mr. J. T. Akiens, junr., decided to take immediate steps to prevent an accident. Overnight he fixed a batten to the leaning pole, and lashed it to the ironwork.

A barrier was erected round a wide area in King Edward Square, and precautions were taken to safeguard the Lord Burton statue.

120 FEET ABOVE BURTON

Next morning a "Burton observer" reporter made the ascent of the steeple, a journey more dirty than perilous. A series of ladders leads up inside the steeple from the Mayors clock – where you clutch at a wire and cause the bell to strike, if you miss your footing.- and out on to a trapdoor about three feet square surrounded by the ornamental railing which is about two feet high.

The flagpole goes into the steeple for some distance and is secured by an iron ring. The fracture has taken place inside this ring and is awkward to reach.

The steeplejack drew up a substantial pole on the outside of the tower and, drawing the broken flagpole back to the perpendicular, they lashed it to the pole and made it secure.

The flagstaff will be demolished by sawing off lengths from the bottom and gradually lowering it through the iron ring. This is likely to prove a ticklish job, as the pole has to remain lashed to its support, yet at the same time the grip of the iron ring has to be freed.

Perched more or less precariously on the railings, I felt quite high enough in the world- writes the Burton Observer reporter- but it was not to be expected Mr Akiens would be content with such a lowly position. He at once swarmed up the flagstaff and continued to lash it to the new support, meanwhile holding on with only one leg. This is literally true.

WHAT, NO TEA

Mr. J. T. Akiens junior, of Burton arrived through the trapdoor like the demon in pantomime, except he didn't look the part. "I've bought the rope," he called.

His uncle was busy within a few feet of the cap on the swaying pole. His cigarette did not seem to be drawing to his satisfaction.

"Yes" he called down, "and I bet you haven't brought the tea. And if you had we haven't got anything to mash it in". What a life

Casting bilious looks over smoky Burton I began the descent, and promptly fell through the clock, you heard the extra quarter of an hour chime shortly before noon, didn't you ? There was no one in the Mayors parlour when I slipped out and made my way into King Edward Place with the same feeling of having done something quite wrong. I glanced up, two or three feet from the top of the pole- say, nearly 160 feet above me- Mr J Akiens appeared to be having trouble with his cigarette. He has decided to change brands.

REMOVING the Burton Town H
flagstaff, which was damaged
gale, and caused alarm throu
threatening to crash to the grou
below. Mr. J. T. Akiens, steep
jack, of Leicester, is seen climb
up the pole. With Mr. J.
Akiens, junr., a little lower,
" Burton Observer " reporter
went to inspect the damage
himself.

Removing the Burton Town Hall flagstaff, which was damaged by a gale, and caused alarm through threatening to crash to the ground below. Mr. J. T. Akiens, steeplejack of Leicester, is seen climbing up the pole. With Mr. J Akiens Junior a little lower, is Burton Observer reporter who went to inspect the damage for himself.

＊＊＊＊＊＊＊＊＊＊＊＊＊＊＊＊＊

150

AN ANCIENT BRETBY LANDMARK, the chimney of the mill, which has had to be demolished owing to its dangerous state. It is estimated to be at least 150 years old, and Mr. Akiens, the well-known Burton steeplejack, had a difficult task taking it down brick by brick.

AN ANCIENT BRETBY LANDMARK, the chimney of the mill, which is has had to be demolished owing to its dangerous state. It is estimated to be 150 years old, and Mr Akiens, the well known Burton steeplejack, had a difficult task taking it down brick by brick.

* * * * * * * * * * * * * * * * *

BURTON STEEPLEJACK'S FEAT.

Re-gilded Weathercock Placed on Pinnacle.

A remarkable feat of skill and nerve was performed on Thursday in Burton. It was unnoticed by more than a dozen or two passers-by. This was not altogether surprising, as it occurred 245 feet above the street level, so that many people walked past without knowing that anything unusual was 'taking place.

Mr J Akiens of Moor Street, a well known steeplejack employed by Messrs. Akiens of Moor Street had the unenviable task of replacing the weather cock on the pinnacle of the Holy Trinity church steeple in Horninglow Street. One of, if not the highest in Burton

The difficulty was not in reaching the top but in pivoting the weather cock which has been re-gilded, on the spindle. Though it Is hard to believe when looking at it from below, that small weather cock weighs half.a hundred weight. Mr. Akiens had to convey it up to the base of the pinnacle and then. holding his position with one hand, he had to lift the cock four feet and balance it on the spindle. In all, Mr. Akiens was aloft 'bout 20 minutes.

Even though this Is the third time that he has accomplished such an undertaking recently (At St. Johns, Horninglow at Repton, in addition to Holy Trinity) Mr Akiens had to admit it had been a tough job. "It was very rough and squally up there " he told a "Burton Observer' Porter who Interviewed him after he had descended. The wind was so troublesome that, to tell you the truth I did not think I should manage it. After the efforts to lift the weathercock, I thought I should have to give it up, but on the third time i managed to place it on the spindle. And take it from me i was glad.

****

Noted Steeplejack`s Death After Accident

JOHN THOMAS AKIENS aged 44, a well known steeplejack, of moor street, died last night at the Burton Infirmary.
He was injured on Thursday when, riding a cycle over the Wetmore Bridge, Burton, he was involved in collision with a motor car. He was picked up with serious head injuries, and never regained consciousness.

Mr. Akiens came from a family of steeplejacks who have done prominent work in the Midlands. His father, Mr. J. T. Akiens is still in business at Leicester, from where Mr. Akiens came to Burton about 10 years ago. He was responsible for most of the big work on the Burton breweries, and was also a contractor for the corporation.

He had frequently carried out hazardous tasks in Derby and other Midland centres. He has had many hairbreadth escapes while at work at dizzy heights. One of his most important jobs was the felling of Bass`s chimney at Shobnall some years ago.
Mr Akiens who was an R. A. O. B. member leaves a widow, two sons and one daughter, who is in Australia. The funeral will take place on Thursday at Christ Church.

****

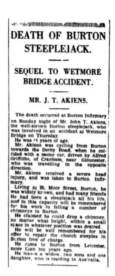

DEATH OF BURTON
STEEPLEJACK.

SEQUEL TO WETMORE
BRIDGE ACCIDENT.

MR. J. T. AKIENS.

The death occurred at Burton Infirmary
on Sunday night of Mr. John T. Akiens,
the well-known Burton steeplejack, who
was involved in an accident at Wetmore
Bridge on Thursday.
He was 44 years of age.
Mr. Akiens was cycling from Burton
towards the Derby Road, when he collided with a motor car, driven by Alfred
Griffiths, of Cranham, near Gloucester,
who was travelling in the opposite
direction.
Mr. Akiens received a severe head
injury, and was taken to Burton Infirmary.
Living at 95, Moor Street, Burton, he
was widely known, and had many friends.
He had been a steeplejack all his life,
and in this capacity will be remembered
for his work in felling a number of
chimneys in Burton.
He claimed he could drop a chimney,
no matter what height, within a small
space in whatever position was desired.
He will be well remembered for his
offer to repair the church steeples in
Burton free of charge.
He came to Burton from Leicester,
more than ten years ago.
He leaves a widow, two sons and one
daughter, who is residing in Australia.

DEATH OF BURTON STEEPLEJACK

SEQUEL TO WETMORE BRIDGE ACCIDENT

MR. J. T. AKIENS.

The death occurred at Burton Infirmary on Sunday night of Mr. John A. Akiene. the well-known Burton steeplejack, who was involved in an accident at Wetmore Bridge on Thursday. He was 44 years of age.

Mr. Akiens was cycling from Burton towards the Derby Road. when he collided with a motor car, driven by Alfred Griffith, of Cranham, near Gloucester, who was travelling in the opposite direction.

Mr. Akiens received a severe head Injury. and taken to Burton Infirmary.

Living at 95, Moor Street, Burton, he was widely known, and had many friends. He had been a steeplejack all his life, and in this capacity will be remembered for his work in felling a number of chimneys in Burton.

He claimed he could drop a chimney, no matter what height, within a small space in whatever position was desired.

He will be well remembered for his offer to repair the church steeples in Burton free of charge.

He came to Burton from Leicester, more than ten years ago. He leaves a widow, two sons and one daughter, who is residing in Australia.

****

Because of the families reputation of being among the best steeplejacks around, they could command higher prices for their work. After Tom Akiens died in the motor accident, other steeplejacks were claiming they worked for the family to get better money. The family heard about this and were not happy at all. Their reputation meant a lot to them.

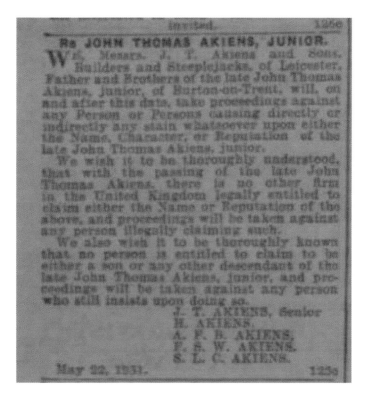

RE. JOHN THOMAS AKIENS JUNIOR.

WE, Messrs. J. T. Akiens and Sons, Builders and Steeplejacks, of Leicester, Father and Brothers of the late John Thomas Akiens Junior, of Burton Upon Trent, will, on and after this date, take proceedings against any person or persons causing directly or indirectly any stain whatsoever upon either the name, character or reputation of the late John Thomas Akiens.

We wish it to be thoroughly understood, that with the passing of the late John Thomas Akiens there is no other firm in the United Kingdom legally entitled to claim either the name or reputation of the above, and proceedings will be taken against any person illegally claiming such.

We also wish it to be thoroughly known that no person is entitled to claim to be either a son or any other descendant of the late John Thomas Akiens junior, and proceedings will be taken against any person who still insists upon doing so.

J.T. Akiens Senior , H. Akiens , A. F. B. Akiens , F. S. W. Akiens , S. C. L. Akiens, (Granddad.)

May 22nd 1931

∗∗∗∗∗∗∗∗∗∗∗∗∗

There were a lot of cowboys about, like this next one who tried to pull a fast one over the vicar.

The Rev W. Bothamley, Rector of St. Leonard's, Exeter, has distinguished himself by climbing the steeple on his church. A steeplejack had declared that the steeple was in a dangerous state at the top, but on the reverend gentleman going up to see for himself he found nothing much amiss.

There are good and bad in every trade I suppose. Like this bloke who worked for the family. He claimed to be J T Akiens of Burton, after he`d died.

156

BURTON STEEPLEJACK'S THEFTS. Story of £20 Cheque.

REPAIR WORK AT HORNINGLOW CHURCH.

A Burton steeplejack was sent to prison by Burton Borough magistrates on Thursday for six months with hard labour, for stealing £20. l9s. 8d. from a Horninglow shopkeeper by means of a cheque signed by the Rev. P.H.Mills. Vicar of Horninglow. The steepiejack. who was working on repair work at Horninglow church, also obtained £1 by false pretences from the vicar, and for that offence was sentenced to a month's Imprisonment, to run concurrently.

The prisoner was Herbert Askey (38) of Moor Street. Burton. On a charge of drunkenness, Askey was fined 10s. He was also ordered to forfeit £1 of his, bail on the drunkenness charge. It was explained that he failed to answer his bail a week ago.

The man from whom Askey admitted baving the £20 19s 8d- Mr William Joseph Moon. of Horninglow Road North, Horninglow, whose shop is opposite Horninglow Parish Church—said Askey, who witness knew as a steeplejack working on the church asked for the loan of £4. In return he offered a cheque signed by the Nev. P. H. Mills, and on this witness gave Askey the £4.

A few days later, Askey came back for the balance of the cheque, and this sum, £16 19s 8d was paid by witness to the prisoner.

Askey endorsed the cheque with the name J. T. Akiens, Jnr.'

VICAR'S EVIDENCE

The Rev. P. H. Mills, vicar of Horninglow, from whom Askey obtained £4 said that on January 5th Askey called at the vicarage, presenting a card with the name J T. Akiens Jnr." on It. Askey presented an estimate for some work on the church, as coming from Akiens.

On March 7th, while Askey was engaged on the work, he asked for 3 or 4 pounds as he had no money for the week-end. Witness offered £1 and asked for a receipt, which Askey signed in the name of Akiens.

But for this representation of Askey being Akiens, the money would not have been given.

Detective-Officer Cooper said that when charged with the first offence Askey said: "It is quite true. I shall do all I can to pay it back in six months—very likely less than that. I have got work to go to.

"CANT CONTRADICT IT"

In reply to the second charge Askey said, "I can`t contradict it. I have had the money." None of the money had been recovered despite a police search of premises in Moor Street. Askey asked if he could pay the money back as soon as possible.

Mrs F. Akiens,of moor street, Burton, the sole proprietor of J. T. Akiens Ltd., said that Askey had been in her employ as a steeplejack for several years, but he had no authority to collect money. He was not her son.

It was on a charge of drunkenness that he was allowed bail to the amount of £2, and when asked why he did not answer the bail, Askey said "I was threatened and dare not come to court last Friday."

Superintendent H. G. Heath: Do you suggest the police threatened you ?

Askey "No, it was a man in the town".

A further charge of obtaining £2 by false pretences, which Askey admitted, was taken into consideration.

Superintendent Heath said Askey was born in London, but had spent most of his life in Derbyshire. Six weeks after he was married his wife left him.

He had held various occupations for short periods, and had been in Burton as a steeplejack for four years.

****

This next article probably did those people who claimed to work for the family a favour, they could have easily been killed attempting to do the kind of work the family did.

> "The younger the child learns to get over his first fear of heights the better it is for him." said Mr. Akiens.
>
> It is not essential to be born into the trade to become a good steeplejack. "I have had some very good lads." Mr. Akiens said of the men who have worked for him. "But mind you they have never been able to do things which we have been able to do." The "we" referred to the family.

"**The younger the child** learns to get over his first fear heights the better it is for him," said Mr. Akiens.

It is not essential to be born into the trade to become a good steeplejack. I have had some very good lads, Mr. Akiens said, of the men who have worked for him. "But mind you, they have never been able to do things which we have been able to do." The "we" referred to the family.

****

159

STEEPLEJACK
DEAD

Oldest at Trade in
the Midlands

MR J. T. AKIENS of Leicester, the oldest steeplejack in the Midlands, who died at his home on Saturday.

STEEPLEJACK DEAD

Oldest at Trade in the Midlands
Mr J. T. Akiens, aged 67, of Payne street, Leicester, the oldest steeplejack in the Midlands, died at his home on Saturday following a short illness.

Mr Akiens, whose family have been steeplejacks for generations, started work when he was seven years old, and up until a few months before he died was still doing special jobs where skill and experience were essential. He had 15 children of his own, but in all he had brought up a family of 24. Mr Akiens held a knowledge of climbing was one of the essential, and consequently he bought up the whole of his family in the art.

Even the girls were not exempt, and sometimes they even helped him in his work, climbing the tallest chimneys with a fearlessness equal to that of their brothers.

SONS HELP :

It was Mr Akiens boast that he never turned down a job, however dangerous. He had innumerable accidents and during his long and strenuous career, he had broken nearly every bone in his body at times.

Often helped by his four sons, Harold, Sidney, Bill and Baden, he carried on his work on the tops of chimneys when the fires below were still alight.

His wife used to help him as well, and once when a high corporation chimney had to be insulated, she lowered her husband over the edge, and held him there with the rope tied around her waist until he had finished the job.

During the war Mr. Akiens and his sons were given the job of keeping the boilers at the Leicester Base Hospital in condition, and several times the clothes were burned off their bodies through having to carry out operations while the fires were banked.

Mr Akiens was a leading member of the St John Ambulance Brigade, and his training in the unit came in useful on many occasions.

Mr Akiens eldest son was killed in a motor accident at Burton a month ago, but his four remaining sons are still carrying on their fathers hazardous trade.

＊＊＊＊＊＊＊＊＊＊＊＊

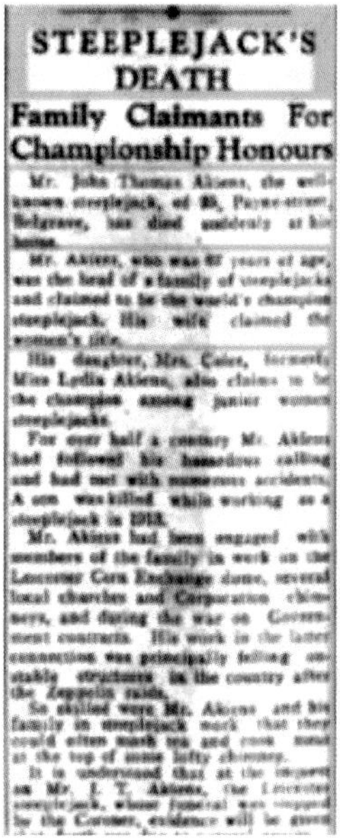

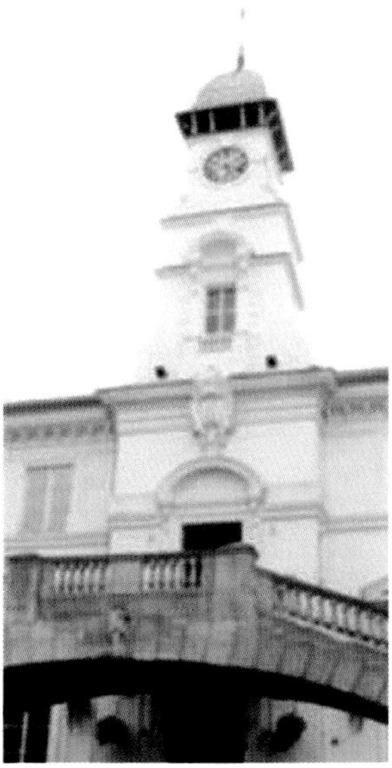

Leicester Corn Exchange

STEEPLEJACK'S DEATH

Family Claimants For Championship Honours

Mr. John Thomas Akiens, the well known steeplejack, of 25, Payne-street, Belgrave, has died suddenly at his home. Mr. Akiens, who was 67 years of age, was the head of a family of steeplejacks and claimed to be the world's champion steeplejack. His wife claimed the women's title.

His daughter, Mrs. Coles, formerly Miss Lydia Akiens, was the champion among junior women steeplejacks. For over half a century Mr. Akiens had followed his hazardous calling and had met with numerous accidents. A son was killed while working as a steeplejack in 1913.

Mr. Akiens had been engaged with members of the family in work on the Leicester Corn Exchange, several local churches and Corporation chimneys, and during the war on Government contracts. His work in the latter connection was principally felling unstable structures in the country after the Zeppelin raids.

So skilled were Mr. Akiens and his family in steeplejack work that they could often mash tea and cook meat at the top of some lofty chimney. It is understood that at the inquest on Mr. J. T. Akiens, the Leicester steeplejack, whose funeral was stopped by the Coroner, evidence will be given that death was due to natural causes.

****

When Great granddad died, freemasons came from all over the country to pay their respects. He was a very well known and respected man in Belgrave. He was a very inventive sort of man. He would make most of the things he needed for the chimneys or steeples in his workshop at the back of the two terraced houses on Payne street the family lived in. Gilded weathercocks, carved capstones, window shutters, he made all kinds of things.

It was said he invented the coupling brackets for scaffolding, but someone else took his idea and a patent was put on it. He reminds me of Dibnah in some ways, but they were very very different men in other ways. Fred was a one

162

man band, whereas great granddad was part of a whole family of steeplejacks. Unlike Fred, Great granddad never ever climbed with a drink in him.

The Rev. D. E. K. Llewelyn, vicar of St. Peter's, Belgrave, told me to-night that he was in the vicarage, changing into his vestments, when the news was brought to him that the funeral was not to be held.

"The news came as a terrible shock to me," he said. "Mr. Akiens was known all over the country as a steeplejack He was an extremely popular man.

He was a very popular well respected man in Belgrave, Leicester, and all over the country a hundred years ago.

When he died it made the headlines all week, partly due to someone making allegations that he was poisoned. The funeral was stopped because of his claims. Something the family didn`t take very well at all. They attacked the bloke and gave him a good hiding, leaving him unconscious in the gutter for nearly a couple of hours with broken bones. He was lucky to get off so lightly. They ended up in court, but the case was thrown out. The man in question was labelled a disgrace to the city of Leicester by the judge, for the slander of a well respected local businessman, and for the grief he caused the family.

LEICESTER FUNERAL STOPPED.

POST MORTEM ON STEEPLEJACK.

MOURNERS WARNED AT LAST MINUTE - CROWDS VAIN WAIT

AT the Eleventh hour the funeral of Mr. J. T. Akiens, Leicesters oldest steeplejack, was stopped this afternoon. A post mortem is to be held. Crowds were outside the church of St. Peters, Belgrave, and choir boys waited for the service to begin. Member of the Royal Antedeluvian Order of Buffaloes had come from distant parts of the country to attend the funeral.

POLICE NOTIFICATION :

A SENSATION was caused in the Belgrave district this afternoon, when the funeral of Mr. J. T. Akiens, Leicesters oldest steeplejack, who lived at Payne street, off Checkitts Road, was stopped in order that a post mortem examination could be held.

Akiens died on saturday, at the age of 67, and the funeral was fixed to take place at St Peters church, Belgrave, this afternoon.

The Leicester Coroner, Mr. E. O. B Fowler, told an Evening Mail representative this afternoon that the funeral was postponed because someone went to the Central Police Station today and alleged that Akiens had died from poisoning.

Members of the family and other mourners wer all assembled at the house when it was announced that instructions had been given for the postponement of the funeral.

Many wreaths were at the house ready to be placed on the hearse and carriages. A message was sent to the undertaker, Mr. Oldershaw, and the carriages were stopped.

In the meantime however, the verger was waiting at the door of St. Peters Church for the arrival of the cortege and the choir boys were all ready for the service. People lined the route to the church and inside the churchyard many were waiting who were carrying flowers.

Among the mourners were many Buffaloes, nine of whom had come from distant parts of the country, including Morecombe Bay, for Mr. Akiens was a prominent member of the order. Mr Akien`s son told the family mourners gathered at the house of the postponement which had been ordered, and that a post mortem was to be held.

CHURCHYARD SENSATION : The news soon reached the crowds gathered near the church, and caused a sensation throughout the neighbourhood, where Mr. Akiens is very well known.

It is understood that the funeral will probably be held tomorrow. At 3.15 this afternoon- three quarters of an hour after the time fixed for the funeral- people were still arriving at the church.

The registrar at the Welford Road cemetery, where the burial was to take place, informed the "Leicester Evening Mail" that the work of opening the grave had begun when about 12 noon he received instructions that the funeral had been postponed.

The operations were at once discontinued and the registrar now awaits permission, before they can be resumed. This he expects to receive tomorrow.

A DAUGHTERS DISTRESS :

A daughter of Mr. Akiens, Mrs. Lydia Cole said everything had been done for her father. She was very distressed and said they had had a lot of trouble. One of her brothers, John Thomas Akiens, was killed in a motor accident at Burton only a few weeks ago.

Mr. S Oldershaw, the undertaker, who was to have carried out the funeral arrangements, said that when he was notified by a detective from the Leicester City Police Force of the postponement at 1.30 today, everything was ready for the funeral, including the coaches and...

****

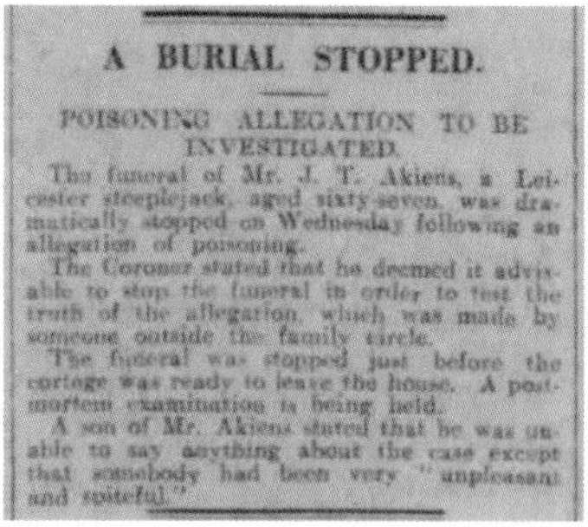

A BURIAL STOPPED : POISONING ALLEGATION TO BE INVESTIGATED.

The funeral of Mr. J. T. Akiens, a Leicester Steeplejack, aged 67 was dramatically stopped on Wednesday following an allegation of poisoning. The Coroner stated that he deemed it advisable to stop the funeral in order to test the truth of the allegation, which was made by someone outside the family circle. The funeral was stopped just before the cortege was ready to leave the house. A post mortem examination is being held. A son or Mr. Akiens stated

166

that he was unable to say anything about the case except that somebody had been very unpleasant and spiteful.

****

STOPPED FUNERAL SEQUEL.

MAN ALLEGES ASSAULT BY RELATIVES.

LEICESTER CASE FAILS.   PROSECUTORS ADMISSIONS :

THE DEFENCE NOT CALLED UPON.

Walter Allen, the man who gave information which resulted in the funeral Mr J. T. Akiens a Leicester steeplejack, being stopped recently, summoned five members of the deceased`s family for assault at Leicester today. The defendants were Baden Akiens, William Akiens, Mrs. Gertrude Thompson, Miss Rose Akiens, and Mrs Lydia Cole. He alleged that they all surrounded him, and all but William struck him. As a result he was unconscious for an hour and a half.
Cross examined, he admitted that at the adjourned inquest the coroner said he was a disgrace to the city. He also admitted a number of convictions, and that he had served various periods of imprisonment. The case was dismissed without calling on the defence.

****

STOPPED FUNERAL DRAMA.

NO TRACE OF POISON IN STEEPLE-
JACK'S BODY.

POST-MORTEM SEQUEL TO
LEICESTER SENSATION.

A post-mortem examination of the body of
Mr. J. T. Akiens, 67, a Leicester steeplejack, whose funeral was stopped yesterday
when 30 mourners were on the point of leaving the house, reveals that death was due to
natural causes.

There was no trace of poison in the body.
A policeman appeared at the house yesterday as the cortege was about to leave, and
informed relatives and friends of the dead
man that the coroner had ordered the funeral
to be stopped, as someone (not a member of
the family) had gone to the Central Police
Station, Leicester, and made the allegation
that Akiens had been poisoned.

STOPPED FUNERAL DRAMA

NO TRACE OF POISON IN STEEPLE-JACKS BODY.

POST MORTEM SEQUEL TO LEICESTER SENSATION :
A post-mortem examination of Mr J. T. Akiens 67, a Leicester Steeple-jack, whose funeral was stopped yesterday when 30 mourners were on the point of leaving the house, reveals that death was due to natural causes.
There was no trace of poison in the body. A policeman appeared at the house yesterday as the cortege was about to leave, and informed relatives and friends of the dead man that the coroner had order the funeral to be stopped, as someone (not a member of the family) had gone to the central police Station Leicester, and made the allegation that Akiens had been poisoned.

＊＊＊＊＊＊＊＊＊＊＊＊＊＊＊＊＊＊

MAN WHO STOPPED FUNERAL

SUMMONSES FOR ALLEGED ASSAULT DISMISSED

A stopped funeral had a police court sequel at Leicester to-day. Walter Allen, of Forest-road, Leicester, summoned Baden Akiens William Akiens, Gertrude Thompson, Rose Akiens, and Lydia Coles for assault. He said that they all set upon him, and a bone in his wrist was broken.

Questioned by Mr. Bennet, on behalf of the defendants, he agreed that he was the man who stopped the funeral of Mr. Akiens on July 4. He denied that at the time he suggested that Mr. Akiens had been poisoned. He was perfectly well aware that he was lying. He agreed that at the inquest, at which a verdict of death from natural causes was returned, the Coroner had said that he was a disgrace to the city.

Evidence was given, and at the close of the case for the complainant the bench dismissed the summonses without calling upon the defence.

MAN WHO STOPPED FUNERAL

SUMMONSES FOR ALLEGED ASSAULT DISMISSED

A stopped funeral had a police court sequel at Leicester today. Walter Allen, of Forest Road, Leicester, summoned Baden Akiens, William Akiens, Gertrude Thompson, Rose Akiens, and Lydia Coles for assault. He said they all set upon him, and a bone in his wrist was broken.
Questioned by Mr. Bennet, on behalf of the defendants, he agreed that he was the man who stopped the funeral of Mr Akienson July 4th. He denied that at the time he suggested Mr. Akiens had been poisoned. He was perfectly well aware that he was lying. He agreed that at the inquest, at which a verdict of death from natural causes was returned, the Coroner had said that he was a disgrace to the city of Leicester.
Evidence was given, and at the close of the case for the complainant the bench dismissed the summones without calling upon the defence.

****

"Coroner Describes Man As "A Disgrace to Leicester"

WIDOW PLEADS PROTECTION : TERRIFIED OF MAN WHO STOPPED CITY FUNERAL

"INVETERATE LIAR"   -says Coroner.

"Your conduct is absolutely disgraceful. You are a disgrace to the city in which you live in, and i don`t want anything more to do with you."

THESE were the words employed at an inquest held last night, by the Leicester Coroner in condemning Mr. Walter Allen, who was responsible for causing the coroner to stop the funeral of Mr. J. T. Akiens, the 67 year old Leicester Steeplejack.

Mr. Allen has stated he believed the dead man had committed suicide by taking poison, and he had heard in Belgrave that he was the cause of it. The Coroner, acting on the evidence of a doctor who conducted the post mortem on Akiens, found death was due to natural causes. Mrs. Akiens, widow of the dead man, then appealed to the Coroner for police protection, saying she was terrified of Allen.

HOPE OF PUNISHMENT : Leicester City Coroner, Mr E. G. B. Fowler, addressed himself in scathing terms to Walter D. A. Allen, the man primarily responsible for the postponement of the funeral of Mr. John Thomas Akiens, the 67 year old steeplejack at last nights inquest on Akiens, which was reported in the later editions of the "Leicester Evening Mail."

It will be recalled that the Coroner held up the funeral just before the cortege was about to leave the dead mans house in Payne street, because Allen stated that he had reason to believe Akiens had committed suicide by taking poison.

After hearing the evidence of Allen who is a brother in law of Akiens, the Coroner said :

"You have uttered a wicked slander against a dead man, and you have put his relatives to much pain and great worry"

" I don`t believe a single word you have said. In my opinion your conduct is absolutely disgraceful : you are a disgrace to the city in which you live. I don`t want anything more to do with you. Your conduct is absolutely abominable, there is no other word for it." Mr Fowler added that he hoped it would be found possible to punish Allen in some way for what he had done. The inquest was held immediately after the burial, Akiens relatives going straight to the town hall from the cemetery.

OPERATION REFUSED : Dr. C. Coyne Elliot, who said he had attended Akiens for chronic gastric trouble for the past eight years, gave evidence that the dead man was subject to bouts of sickness, accompanied by intense pain.

He had been recommended to have an operation but persistently refused. Dr Elliot was called to him last Friday, when he had a much more serious attack than usual.

The Coroner " Was there anything to suggest that the cause was anything other than natural ?" -Nothing. Dr Elliot said Akiens condition be.....(continued)

WHY WITNESS WENT TO THE POLICE : Dr. Elliot said Akiens condition became worse on the Friday afternoon, and he suggested an immediate operation, but his patient would not hear of it. On the following morning he was in a collapsed condition, and nothing could be done for him then, and he died. The doctor was satisfied as to the cause of death and issued a certificate.

The Coroner : There was nothing in his symptoms to indicate he might have had poison ? - No.

There was no suggestion made to you by any of his relatives that he might have taken poison ? - No.

You knew nothing of the suggestion prior to Wednesday ? - No

Dr. Elliot made a post mortem examination on Wednesday and found nothing to indicate poisoning. Death was due to rupture of the stomach caused by gastric ulcers.

The Coroner : A man named Allen came to you about noon on Wednesday, didn`t he ? - Yes

Did you tell him that you thought the family were keeping something from you ? -No.

I did not expect you to say yes, but i had to put it to you. He suggested that Mr. Akiens had died from poisoning, didn`t he ? - Yes. That was the first time i had heard that suggestion.

172

The widow Mrs. Ellen Akiens, corroborated that her husband would not hear of an operation.

"WOULD NOT OWN HIM"

The Coroner : Has any member of your family made any suggestion of the possibility that your husband might have taken poison ? - No.

Do you know of any reason for any suggestion of the sort being made ? - No

There is a man named Allen; is he any relation ? - He is a brother in law of my husband, who would not own him. I should not know him if i saw him.

Alfred F. B. Akiens, a son of the dead man, said that his father was taken ill while out with him on Friday.

From that time until his death he had nothing else but water, a little Brandy, meat extract, and the doctors medicine, said Mr. Akiens. He had never made any threats to take his life, and he was in good financial circumstances.

The Coroner : Have you since heard that allen said in the Belgrave working mens club on Sunday that there would be no funeral on Wednesday ?

I have heard that since.

Events culminating in the last minute stoppage of the funeral were related by sergt. Lyner, who said Allen came to the police station on Wednesday morning and said he would like to see sergt. Jenney, the Coroners officer. That was at a quarter to one.

Allen said "I am acting as a private enquiry agent for solicitors acting on behalf of claimants to property known as Thurlaston estates" Said sergt.Lyner.

He wanted the funeral stopped. He said " I have had an interview with Dr. Elliot this morning, and although he has issued a certificate he thought at the time the family were keeping something from him."

"Allen also said that members of the family had told him that the dead man had drunk a tumbler of a white liquid, about an hour before he died, and said " im done."

Sergt. Lyner added that Allen told him that he knew Mr. Akiens had on five previous occasions attempted to commit suicide.

The Coroner recalled Mr. Akiens son and asked : Is there any truth in the suggestion that your father has tried to commit suicide on five previous occasions ? - None whatever, answered Mr Akiens.

Walter Douglas Arthur Allen had said he was a motor engineer and gave his address as forest road, Leicester, admitted making a statement to the Police, in which occurred the passage :

" I have reason to believe that he (Akiens) might have committed suicide. His wife and other members of the family suggested he had taken something during Saturday morning, and they said that i had been the cause of it. I have no idea of what he might have taken."

The Coroner : What reason had you to believe that he might have committed suicide ? - His own family said so on Saturday night to two of his sisters.

Were you there ? - No

Well how do you know what they said ? - They came to see me at my house. They told me it was said by Caroline Suffolk, his daughter, that it was the miles and the cochranes money that caused it..

Why do you suggest that his wife and other members of the family suggested that he may have taken something ? It was said by Caroline Suffolk. She came running into the house and said my fathers taken something. Its the money that`s caused his death. You know all about it. That was the reason i came and made the statement. I heard in Belgrave on Sunday that i was the cause of this death.

What do you mean by saying that the doctor told you that he thought the family were keeping something back ? - The doctor thought probably they would have been keeping something back.

He didn`t say anything of the sort. Why did you tell sergt. Lyner that ? It was a lie - I made the statement to the doctor. If it is said that i told the seargent, then that`s my mistake.

174

The Coroner again read the statement and said " It is an absolute falsehood"

Allen : I never made the statement.

The Coroner : Then you are suggesting that sergt. Lyner was not putting down the truth ? - No. It was either a mistake on my part or the sergeants.

The Coroner : It is an absolute lie. I don`t believe a single word you have said. I don`t believe there is a single word of truth in this suggestion about poisoning, or anything else you have said.

In summing up, Mr Fowler said Allen had uttered a wicked slander against a dead man, and had put his relatives to much trouble and great worry. " In my opinion," the Coroner went on, " Your conduct is absolutely disgraceful. You are a disgrace to the city in which you live, and i don`t want anything more to do with you."

" I am very grieved for the relatives in this case. I was informed less than two hours before the funeral of a statement by this man- who seems to me to be an inveterate liar- which had been given to the police. In the interests of justice it was necessary that the question should be settled and i ordered the funeral to be stopped.

"I am perfectly satisfied by the post mortem that the death of Mr. Akiens was due to natural causes, and that there is no evidence whatever of his having taken poison. I am also quite satisfied that there is no foundation for this wicked suggestion made by Allen on the flimsiest of grounds.

His conduct is abominable. There is no other word for it. I do hope that it will be found possible to punish him in some way for what he has done.

The Coroner recorded a verdict that death was due to natural causes.

There was another sensation after the verdict for the widow appealed to the Coroner for police protection. " I didn`t know this man was Allen until now, " said Mrs. Akiens, " But he has been about my house since Sunday.

The Coroner promised that the police would attend to the matter.

****

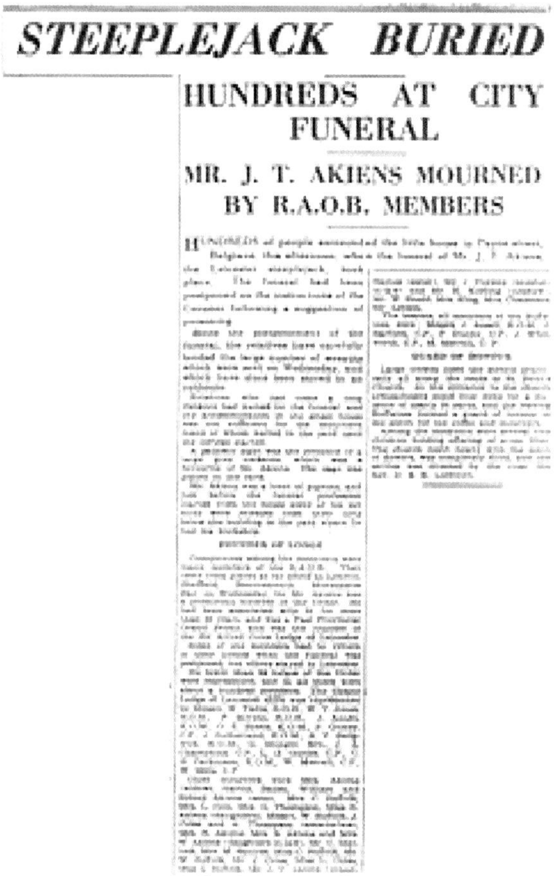

STEEPLEJACK BURIED

HUNDREDS AT CITY FUNERAL

MR. J. T. AKIENS MOURNED BY R.A.O.B. MEMBERS

STEEPLEJACK BURIED

HUNDREDS AT CITY FUNERAL

Mr J. T. AKIENS MOURNED BY R.A.O.B MEMBERS

Hundreds of people surrounded the little house on Payne Street, Belgrave, this afternoon, when the funeral of Mr J. T. Akiens, the Leicester Steeplejack, took place. The funeral had been postponed on the instruction of the Coroner following a suggestion of poisoning.

Since the postponement of the funeral, the relatives have carefully tended the large number of wreaths which were sent on Wednesday, and which have since been stored in an outhouse.

Relatives who had come a long distance had waited for the funeral, and the accommodation in the small house was not sufficient for the mourners, many of whom waited in the yard until the cortege started. A pathetic sight was the presence of a large Grey Cockatoo, which was a favourite of Mr. Akiens. The cage was placed in the yard.

Mr Akiens was a lover of pigeons, and just before the funeral procession started from the house some of his pet birds were released from their lofts below the building in the yard where he had his workshop.

FOUNDER OF THE LODGE : Conspicous among the mourners were many members of the R.A.O.B. They came from places as far afield as Sheffield, Bournemouth, Morecambe Bay, on Wednesday, for Mr Akiens was a prominent member of the Order. He has been associated with it for more than 30 years, and was a Grand Primo, and was founder of the Sir Alfred Coles Lodge of Leicester.

Some of the members had to return to their homes when the funeral was postponed, but others stayed in Leicester.

No fewer than 54 lodges of the order were represented, and in all there were about a hundred members. The Grand Lodge of Leicestershire was represented by...

Chief mourners were Mrs. Akiens (widow), Harold, Baden, William and Sidney Akiens (sons) Mrs. C. Suffolk, Mrs. L. Cole, Mrs. G. Thompson, Miss R. Akiens (daughters) Messrs. Mr. W. Suffolk, J. Coles, and A. Thompson (sons in law), Mrs H. Akiens, Mrs. B Akiens, and Mrs. W. Akiens (daughters in law), Mr. C. Matlock, Mrs. M. Squires, Miss C Suffolk, Mr W Suffolk, Mr. J. Coles, Miss L. Coles, Miss I. Suffolk, Mr. J. T. Akiens (Grand children)

The bearers were all members of the Buffaloes.

Large crowds lined the streets practically all along the route to St. Peters Church. At the entrance to the church sympathisers stood four deep for a distance of nearly 30 yards, and the leading Buffaloes formed a guard of honour in the porch for the coffin and mourners. Among the mourners were several tiny children holding offering of Arum Lillies. The church itself, heavy with the scent of flowers, was completely filled, and the service was directed by the vicar, the Rev. D. E. K. Llewelyn.

****

The funeral finally leaving Payne street in Belgrave, led out by members of the freemasons the R.A.O.B. Even after all those years Granddad was still angry about the events surrounding his dads funeral.

J. T. AKIENS & SONS

BUILDERS & ORIGINAL

STEEPLE CLIMBERS

LEICESTER

This photo was taken around 1925/26. Pictured from left to right is Granddad sitting cross legged, Sid, (Sidney Clarence Laurence), behind him standing is Frank Samuel William, (Bill) Alfred Frederick Baden, (Baden) standing and Harold Sitting, with Great granddad standing further back on the right. John Thomas junior had already moved to Burton a few years before this photo was taken. Why half of them took different names to the ones they were given I have no idea. I think a lot of families did that in those days. One thing that I notice about this photo is that granddad has all his fingers. Another thing I notice is the size of his hands, and his knuckles. Hes barely a teenager.

179

Photo A Melbourne

Granddad as i remember him. Sidney Clarence Laurence Akiens, born October 12th 1912. He told me so many stories from that era, it was a very different way of life. After my Dad, he was the most remarkable man ive ever met, they broke the mold when they made him. He never stole a thing from anyone his whole life, that was something he told me quite often. After Dad died I spent a lot of time with him going over all the stories of how life was for him growing up being a part of this family. He would sit for hours telling me all the stories about some of the things he got up to. From as long as i can remember, granddad was always telling us stories.

Its fair to say he was known in the family for telling tall stories, that people found hard to believe. Like the story of taking new born babies to the top of chimneys, people doubted that but it turned out that it was true. When we were kids we weren`t bothered if they were true or not. It was great hearing them. If any of them weren`t true, then he must have had one hell of an imagination dreaming them up. Dad told a lot of stories as well, it seems to run in the family, in my case i write them.

Service Steeplejacks, the business Granddad started after he fell out with one of his brothers, he felt he was pushed out of the family business. No.1 Duchess street Belgrave. They performed a very different kind of service high above the services the vicars performed in the church. At one time Grandad had a dozen or so blokes working for him. One lad of 18 was unloading the scaffolding from the lorry one day when a dog ran into the road. A driver swerved to miss it and drove into the back of the lorry. A scaffold bar went through the young lads chest, he died a few days later in hospital. Dad was very upset by it, the lad was like a big brother to him.

Me and Granddad in the back yard of Duchess street in Belgrave in 1970. You can just about see his missing thumb and two smaller fingers on his right hand. Below, granddad beside the motorbike that apparently won one of the early TT races. This could have been the bike he nearly died on. The accident that nearly saw him burnt alive didn`t put him off speed.

When they were working on the chimney at Nabisco Frears in Wigston, they could see grass snakes swimming across the river from where they worked. Granddad went down and caught one of them. The van was off the road for some reason so they had to go home on the bus. He had the snake in a biscuit tin with brown paper and an elastic band covering the top. Dad refused to sit anywhere near him, it must have been very worried with the smell it was giving off, it stunk the whole bus out. It farted all the way home. When he got it home it escaped in the house. My aunt told me, "I had eyes like bloody dinner plates for two days, two whole days" she told me, "until your granddad caught the pissing thing."

Lauren Mary Akiens, my daughter who we named after dad, and me and my aunt who had eyes like dinner plates for two days. She is the last one of all the girls that climbed chimneys (in our line). She taught me what colours were what. We were down Grandma and Granddads one day when I was about 4 or 5. She had a bag of foxes glacier fruits. She told me what all the colours were. She said I could have each sweet if I got the colour right. I didn't get a single one wrong. Then she said, well done Scott, now come and give you`re Aunt Jacky a kiss. I said, " Hang on, that wasn't part of the deal, no one said anything about that". I got the sweets.

My uncle told me this story about granddad on fb.

Love the photo of Dad standing on his head, something I never quite managed to do. I remember him doing it one night when he'd came back from the hotel Belgrave. He went up stairs to bed, realised the gussunder in the bedroom needed emptying so he decided to do it. As we sat down stairs we heard an almighty racket behind the door for the stair way. When we opened the door, there dad was, upside down with his arse in the air and the half full Jerry upright in his hand. He'd tripped coming down the stairs and landed upside down, without spilling much. If it had been a pint of beer I'm sure he would not have spilt any. We all laughed about that for years.

The motorbike accident didn`t put him off motorbikes, cars or trucks. If anything, it probably made him worse, he lived through being half burnt alive. It would explain a lot if that accident made him feel invincible. He learnt to drive in a flat bed truck. It had a wrench bolted on to where the steering wheel should be. He used to go scrambling in it over waste ground with his brothers somewhere down Bath street in Belgrave. He didn`t have to pass his test, he got given a driving licence when he was 14. I can totally believe that !

I know from experience, i`ve been on a long journey with him. From Leicester to the SAS headquarters at Sterling lines at Hereford for a family do. It was very eventful. Dad went in another car and told me to sit with granddad to "keep an eye on him". He would`ve been nearly 80 at the time. His car was a bright Orange Allegro estate. It was a good job it was bright orange, at least people stood a slim chance of seeing him, before he suddenly shot past and cut in front of them.

He could only just see over the steering wheel. I`ve never experienced anything like it in a car, never been as scared and laughed so much at the same time in my whole life. Bearing in mind he was only holding the steering wheel with two fingers. His left hand was permanently on the gear stick, always ready to drop down a gear, so he could go flying past another unsuspecting driver, scaring them half to death as he cut them up.

He seemed to have his own highway code. Red lights seemed optional, depending on the traffic. If there wasn`t anything coming, we kept going. I could see he was going to run a red light, but i couldn`t tell him for laughing. When i did manage to tell him as we shot through one red light, he just said, "aaah balls to it", or something similar. He told me how he must have made that journey a hundred times or more. Which surprised me a bit, we got lost twice.

Granddad was casually chatting about all the jobs he`d worked on along the way, as we hurtled along. "I worked on that, pointed that, painted that." He was looking up nearly as much as he was looking at the road. The motorway was especially memorable, i`m still amazed to this day we got off it alive. He just carved people up and went in whatever lane he needed, to get by whoever was in the way. I was surprised he didn`t go up the hard shoulder. I don`t think he bothered indicating too much, i lost count of how many people papped their horns at us. Other road users were basically ba*tard nuisances that got in his way. It was made funnier because he wasn`t foul mouthed at all. He was when he was behind the wheel of that car. His granddaughters certainly never heard him speak like that, but he was different with us lads. It was like he was in a race with every other driver on the road, but they didn`t know it.

As we came over the brow of Fromes hill i looked down the steep long road in front of us. I thought my number was up, going by what i`d already witnessed from that passenger seat. He was actually accelerating to overtake cars, in the oncoming lane. I had eyes like bloody dinner plates this time, coming down that hill. It must have been fear that kept them frozen open. Lucky for Granddad there weren`t many speed cameras about at that time, because he`d have got all 12 points needed for a ban on that journey alone. It was more like a cannonball run, than a leisurely drive to visit relatives. When we got there dad asked me how the journey went. He was grinning at me when he asked me. He knew what it would be like, and he didn`t warn me. I felt like kissing

the tarmac. I just said "Well, ive never heard him use the f word til today".
Dad just laughed.

Pictured below, great uncle Bill, the baby, young Sid and Granddad pictured right in the photo taken at a studio on Abbey park road in Leicester in the 1930`s.

They look more like gangsters than demolition men.

We were never too sure if Dad was winding us up. He used to tell me stories of when they worked together, he repeated a lot of what granddad told me. Im not saying the stories were true, im saying its true they told me them. Most have turned out to be true so im inclined to believe the others probably were.

When he was a lad Granddad used to dive into the river Soar from the old iron green bridge at the bottom of Holden street in Belgrave, and swim to the White Horse in Birstall, then he would swim back. He gave me some great advice when I was learning to swim.

At some of the factories dad and granddad worked on, they had vermin in the boiler houses. Wild stoats, ferral cats, rats, all sorts. The big blokes in the boiler suits would be too scared to go in. Dad loved it when this happened. He'd tell them he'd fetch the man who could sort it out. Granddad had a way with animals. He`d walk in and a few minutes later he'd walk out with whatever was in there sitting in his hand. I don't think any of them ever bit him, but he probably wouldn't have felt it if they did because his hands were so hard from the fire and from their work.

He loved all animals, except cats that shit in the flower beds he grew for Grandma. If he came across an injured bird he would bring it home to make it better. He`d feed it bread dipped in milk on the end of a matchstick and bits of worm. When it was well enough he`d let it go. He once caught a fox when he was a lad near to where our house was later built on Stocking farm. He just wanted to have a look at it. They worked on one job repairing the roof of a house, and the owners had a great big dog that looked like a wolf. It slunk across the ground like a wolf, it howled like a wolf. No one could go near it except for the couples little girl. They used to slide the sash window up at the back of the house to feed it. Granddad just walked straight in the back yard showing it no fear at all, held his hand out to it and said "What up wi you then you big silly bleeder", and the dog instantly got on with granddad.

A local Leicester newspaper was running a story called friends and neighbours in Belgrave people in 1957. They wrote about several notable local characters.

This is what they wrote about granddad, after they caught up with him in the Bulls head. They took this photo, and it was all recently re-published online on the Leicester Mercury website. Nice to see my Dad get a mention.

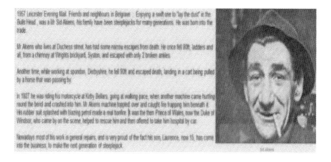

186

1957 Leicester Evening Mail : Friends and neighbours in Belgrave.

Enjoying a swift one to "lay the dust" in the Bulls Head, was Mr Sid Akiens, his family have been steeplejacks for many generations, he was born into the trade.

Mr Akiens who lives at Duchess street, has had some narrow escapes from death. He once fell 80 feet, ladders n` all from a chimney at Wrights brickyard, Syston, and escaped with only two broken ankles.

Another time while working at Spondon Derbyshire, he fell 90 feet, landing in a cart being pulled by a horse, that was passing by.

In 1927 he was riding his motor cycle at Kirby Bellars, going at walking pace, when another machine came hurtling round the bend and crashed into him. Mr Akiens machine toppled over and caught fire trapping him beneath it. His rubber suit splashed with blazing petrol made a real bonfire. It was the then Prince of Wales, now the Duke of Windsor, who came by on the scene, helped to rescue him and then offered to take him hospital by car.

Nowadays most of his work is general repairs, and is very proud of the fact his son, Laurence, now 15, has come into the business, to make the next generation of steeplejack.

＊＊＊＊＊＊＊＊＊＊＊＊＊＊＊＊＊

Granddad was the least racist person iv ever met, he would talk to anyone. Anyone willing to listen to his stories and have a laugh. He didn`t care what colour you were or what you looked like. He once said to me, i don`t care what colour people are, There`s good and bad in every race, but arseholes come in all colours, that's what you have to look out for.  If they`re ok with me, im ok with them. I guess that was maybe because he spent years badly scarred and maybe felt ostracised after the motorbike accident. He had bald patches on his head where his hair never grew back, so he wore a hat most of the time. He introduced his eldest daughter to a young Indian bloke he played darts or dominoes with in the pub. They were happily married for the rest of their lives. They took me on holiday when I was 5. My older brother was always getting to go and stay with different aunts and uncles, but no one wanted me round their houses because I was such a little shit, I couldn't be

187

trusted. I remember sitting on my bed crying about it one day. Dad told my aunt who married the Indian man and before you know it, I was on my way to Mablethorpe with them for a couple of weeks. I loved it. Dad even gave me a tenner for spending money. Because of that holiday iv never been racist either.

This was another time Granddad made the papers.

> Then there's steeplejack Sid Aliens, who no doubt had nine lives, but has lost three of them —one when he was trapped under a blazing motor cycle. He was rescued by the Prince of Wales. On two other occasions he fell 80 and 90 feet, and lived to tell the tale.

Dads cousin told me granddad would get him and dad to punch him in the stomach as hard as they could to try and make him flinch. They would be about 12 or 13. They never could, they only hurt their hands and wrists trying. " He was such a hard bleeder your granddad was, completely fearless to everything" he said. He wasn`t afraid of anything, except possibly the tax man.

He had his "fair share of run ins with those buggers" he told me. Dad joked that he was infamous down the tax office". When his tax returns were due, you could find him down there, kicking off, disputing the amount he had to pay. He knew "every trick in the book". Dads way of saying he was a very shrewd man. He showed me one of his tricks in the pub one night.

I was in the Broadway pub playing pool and granddad was at the bar as usual. As we were standing there, he called the landlord over. "Whats up Sid" he asked ? "There`s water in that beer" he replied. There`s no water in that beer he protested. Granddad argued there was. The landlord pulled another pint of mild, took a swig, and gave it to him to taste. Again, he said "There`s water in that one". The landlord said again that it didn`t, then disappeared. He came back 5 or 10 minutes later, as he was finishing the free pint the landlord had given him. He said "I`ve been and changed the barrel Sid, i can promise you there is no water in that beer". He gave him another pint and asked him to taste it. Granddad took a long swig, thought about it, then put the pint on the bar. He said "There`s water in that one as well".The landlord by now was getting a bit annoyed and told him again. "Sid, iv just changed the barrel, there can`t possibly be any water in that beer". Granddad just casually replied, " Well

188

how do they make it then, without water ? ". The landlord just shook his head as he walked off. Granddad winked at me and said, "They all fall for that one". Then cheerfully carried on supping his second free pint.

Another story I remember being told a few times, not just by granddad. A few in the family told me, a very believable story knowing granddad. He broke his big toe at work. He went to the hospital to have it set and after a couple of weeks he noticed they`d set it wrong, it was turned in. His sister Gertrude was there and she suggested he went back back to the hospital. He said "No, they ballsed it up last time, im not bothering with them again." So he set about sorting it out himself. He sat down and actually broke his own toe with his bare hands. Gertrude fainted when the bone snapped. It`s hard to imagine anyone being able to do that, but Granddad was very old school, he always just got on with whatever needed to be done.

He didn't have much time for hospitals or doctors, he maybe thought he knew better than them a lot of the time. You couldn't blame him. When he was a young man he had stomach problems, so the doctors at the hospital thought it was due to his teeth for some strange reason. So they whipped them all out in one go, using pre-war dentistry methods. They took them all out for no reason, he still had the stomach problems, but they sorted themselves out in time.

I managed to get a video recorder and a load of blank tapes for granddad. Someone was flogging it in the pub, so I thought of granddad with just his 4 channels. I dropped it off and said i'd nip back and set the clock and show him how it all worked. I thought he could tape the rugby, the F1 and nature programs. When I went back the next day he'd sorted it all himself, he`d set the clock, and was watching what he'd already recorded the night before. With no instructions at all, it didn't even have the remote control.

Granddad told me this story a few times and it never changed. I don`t know if this one was true, im not saying it was, but it was a great story to hear when we were kids, it made me laugh. He said he fell from a chimney one day in Derbyshire somewhere, and as luck should have it a horse and cart just happened to be passing. It was full of hay and granddad was heading straight for it head first, what a stroke of luck. I can imagine the relief he felt seeing that soft landing rushing up at him, when otherwise it would have meant almost certain death. However, that relief was very short lived. It wasn`t full of hay at all, it was full of pig shit. The hay was covering it to keep the smell down, that`s what they did in those days. But it saved his life. Even if he did break most of his ribs and punctured a lung. When he landed he took all four wheels off the cart. After all that, when he got to the hospital, none of the doctors and nurses wanted to go near him, for some strange reason. He used to chuckle when he told me that story.

I was in the Broadway one Saturday night, standing at the end of the bar with granddad in his usual spot. He would have been 79, maybe a bit older. The Belgrave rugby team were in there celebrating a win. The bell went for last orders and the rugby lads were virtually climbing over each other to get another couple of drinks each. One of them, one of the forwards, bumped into granddad, making him spill his pint. I saw the look on granddads face and thought, oh shit. Without even looking round, he put his pint on the bar, then drew his bent arm forward with a clenched fist, then brought it back as fast and hard as he could, elbowing the rugby lad full in the ribs. Then he just casually picked his pint up, without evening looking round to see who he`d just assaulted. The rugby players head spun round instantly, and saw it was granddad, this little old man. I remember the shocked look on his face as he clutched his ribs. He literally moved the whole pack up the bar away from him. I imagine he didn't take any notice of much worse happening to him during the game, but he took notice of granddad.

A fight broke out in there one night, they were throwing pool balls at each other. The walls were full of circular dents afterwards. Granddad just stood watching it a few feet away, not bothered at all if a pool ball came his way. A cousin of mine had to pull him behind one of the concrete posts in the pub, which he wasn't happy about.

Granddad had a good amatuer boxing career, but he fought with gloves on. It probably wouldn`t have been a fair fight, if it was bare knuckle with how hard his hands were. He didn't need the comical horseshoe in his glove. He had skin like leather on his hands, his knuckles were like rows of elbows. He was a sparring partner for someone who fought for a big title. Quite a few in the family went into boxing, my brother and a couple of my cousins did. They had an Akiens cup at the Belgrave working mens club, awarded to the most improved Junior fighter. The club was very well known for its boxing, Tony Sibson was probably their most famous boxer, he fought for a world title against Marvin Hagler. The display cabinets were full of trophies. My sister asked dad when she was little who won them all. He said he did, all except one. He kept that wind up going for years, she was about 15 before she realised he was bullshitting.

He had 12 fights with only one loss, to someone who was being made to fight inspite of not being a well man. According to Granddad he went easy on him and was duped, the other man won. He gave up boxing after that. These were his gloves. When dad was a kid granddad taught him to box. He would be sparring with him on his knees in the front room. The bull terrier they had used to nip granddad on the arse to get him to stop. The only sport Granddad enjoyed really was Rugby, he had trials for England when he was 12. He didn't have time for football. Neither did dad, he never played it as a kid. They thought footballers were a bunch of big jessies, kissing each other after they scored and getting their hairs permed, who ran about chasing a ball, looking like dogs in the park from where the worked. They said footballers wouldn't do their job for their money, let alone what dad and granddad earned.

They had a few different dogs when my dad was growing up. A great big Alsation called king. Granddad would tell the dog "grumble king" and he growled. He would carry a full house brick in his mouth for miles when they took him out for a walk along the river to Birstall. They had an Airedale terrier that died from his injuries after killing two Labradors that attacked the child of a neighbour. Another dog they had was Toby, a mongrel, the kids in the street used to call for him to come and play war games. They`d put notes in the dogs collar and send him to the other side with messages.

The most memorable one for me was the white English bull terrier granddad picked up from Coventry when he was working there during the blitz. They called him Pete, he was a wire haired mongrel looking dog, you couldn`t tell he was a bull terrier. He went everywhere with dad when he was a nipper.

Granddad worked away for months at a time during the war and when he came home Pete would have forgotten him. One day when he came home from working away for 6 months, my aunt was sitting on his knee when the dog came in from the back yard. Pete didn`t recognise granddad and attacked him. They had one hell of a fight. Granddad got bitten very badly, i saw the scars on his forearms over 40 years later. Neither would back down. Granddad ended up leaving the dog for dead in the back yard. Sometime later the dog managed to drag himself into the house where granddad cleaned him up. From that moment on they had a complete respect for each other. Granddad knew his family would be safe while he was working away with Pete in the house.

They used to call them devil dogs years ago my granddad told me. They were known as the gladiators of the canine race. He certainly earned his keep when it came to guarding the house. When dad was 9, someone poisoned the dog. It broke both dad and granddads hearts. Granddad never did find out who was responsible, it was a good job really. Im sure he would have been up court for murder if he did. When Pete was buried he had a solid silver cross around his neck, because they thought so much of him.

I fell in love with the breed because of all the stories i heard from dad and granddad about this dog. Not because he was nasty, but because he was so loyal and would have died for the family. I went on to have my own White English bull terrier, he was nothing like the stereotypical Bill Sykes dog they had, but he was as amazing. The he was ever attack, was a Avery good mate thought so much he has him his arm, he`s even own dog after the

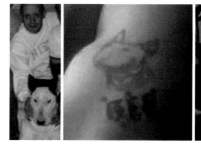

every bit only thing allowed to football. of mine of my dog, tattooed on named his dog I had.

My mates told me i should call him Tyson or Zues, something mean sounding. I named him after the man who gave me that dream as a kid, I called him Sid.

Iv got loads of stories to tell about this dog, i`ll be writing about those in the next book im sure. Here`s one that id like to add to this book though.

192

My Mam rang me at work one day. She said I needed to come home, its Sid. He was only 8 months old at the time. Whats wrong with him I asked. "He`s had bills mountain bike in the back yard, he wont let us take it off him", Mam said. Bill was mams then boyfriend. I said "Why did the daft twat leave his bike in Sids back yard". When I got home the little devil was happily swinging it round like a dinky toy. The tyres were chewed off it, the handle grips, the pedals and the seat. The wheels were buckled like figure eights. He completely destroyed it. All his gums were bleeding, but his tail was wagging like helicopter blades. Bill told me I owed him a new bike, I told him to get stuffed, it was his own fault for leaving it where he did, hadn't he lost enough shoes to know what would happen to the bike.

Me and Sid in the doorway of St. Peters church, Belgrave.

Granddad told us about when he was walking home from the Belgrave working mens club one night to their house in Martin street. It was around 1977, granddad would`ve been about 65 years old at the time. As he was crossing Cossington reccy, a large chap approached him from behind and said, "Give me your wallet old man." Granddad didn`t give him his wallet. He spun round and gave him a good crack on the chin. He was still lying unconscious on the ground as granddad reached the other side of the park.

When we were kids we asked him how he lost his thumb, he told us it was because he picked his nose so much. He was just trying to stop us from picking our noses. He would put the stump to his nostril and make out his thumb was right up his nose. We found it funny at that age.

He had a kettle he used to boil on the stove, it had one of those old whistles to let you know when it was boiling. There was a cloth wrapped around the handle for when it got too hot to touch the metal. You couldn`t touch it for more than a second or two. Granddad wasn`t bothered, he would pick it up just the same if the cloth was on or off. He`d stand there holding it while he was chatting casually away. He couldn't feel either cold or the heat in his hands, he said the nerves must have been burnt away in the accident when he was 15.

Granddad grew all his own veg in the back yard, he certainly had green fingers. He grew runner beans, tomatoes, carrots, onions, cabbages, radishes, lettuces, rhubarb, strawberries, just about everything. He grew a flower bed for grandma outside the window. He also kept ducks and rabbits for the family to eat, a lot of people did back then. The kids would be playing with an animal one day and be horrified to find out they`d just ate it the next day. On one occasion granddad selected a duck they would be having for dinner and took it in the outside toilet where the kids couldn`t see what he did to make them ready for the pot.

He`d hold it upside down with the head between his knees and sharply pull the ducks body upwards. It didn`t quite go to plan this particular day. The duck had other ideas about leaving him with a parting gift. A minute or two later they heard granddad shouting, "You dirty little bastard". Then he appeared in the doorway covered in duck shit, all over his face and in his hair. Everyone thought that was funny, even granddad laughed when he told me the story, but I bet he didn't laugh at the time.

I remember he cooked a mean roast chicken with all the trimmings, I used to go down there on Sundays for dinner when I was a teenager. He once caught a pike and had it in the old Belfast sink with both the tail and head overhanging out of the sides. He salted it for 24 hours and said it was very nice. He could cook almost anything I think. He used to buy conger eel and octopus from the fish market in town. I enjoyed both, but it was only years later that I realised he probably picked those because he had no teeth.

He`d get a goose and fatten it up all year for the family on Christmas day. One day the coalman turned up at their house on Duchess Street, to drop a few bags of coal off. Pete came charging up the back yard going berserk. The coalman had no choice but to dive in the outside toilet to get out of his way. He didn`t know grandma had put the goose in there while she let Pete out in the back yard. Dad said in hindsight, the bloke should have taken his chances with the dog, the goose pecked his arse red raw.

Grandad and Grandma with dad and two of my aunts walking along the front at Mablethorpe or Chapel St. Leonards in 1946/47. This was taken before another aunt and uncle were born. Already by this age dad was climbing chimneys over a hundred feet tall.

Iv often wondered what it must have been like to climb chimneys. Imagining going up rung by rung. What would it have felt like standing on the top of it, seeing everything on the ground looking so small. Feeling it swaying in the wind, with the whole thing rocking, if it was broken through the middle. It would be the wind trying to blow you off it that would make it feel real to me. To imagine looking straight down, hundreds of feet. It would turn my stomach at the thought of it. And then to imagine you`re only 5 years old.

He told me he always had a great sense of freedom when he was high up on chimneys or steeples, birds would fly around them as they worked. I doubt the poor children who went off to work in factories had that same feeling of freedom in their hellish workplaces.

My aunt who wasn`t born when this photo was taken told me only the other week, of when granddad took her up a chimney when she was a little girl aged 4 or 5, if that. It was before she started school she remembers that. She would be on the ladders with granddads arms either side of her as they went up. If she fell she would fall into his body and he was always ready to grab her. Grandma was at the bottom of the chimney having kittens almost, shouting, "Bring her down Sid, she`ll fall." Granddad just shouted back, " No she won`t", and carried on climbing right to the top. It was an experience she will never forget my aunt said.

I remember down Martin street dad and granddad would come back from the pub across the road on a Sunday afternoon, after having 3 or 4 pints. Granddad was about 65 years old at the time, would stand with feet apart and his arms wide and challenge us to try and move his arms. Me and my brothers would be swinging off him and climbing all over him. We couldn`t budge him, he was so solid, muscular and strong for a man his age. He walked a little bow legged, probably from a lifetime of climbing ladders. To us kids he was invincible. He would play fight with us and poke us in the ribs with his finger, the louder we laughed the more he did it. It felt like someone had lobbed a stone at you.

Grandma came from a respectable quite well to do family, they had a chain of grocery shops. They lived on St Margarets place next to St Margarets church close to Leicester town centre. Her family were dead against her and granddad getting together. Even though they lived a mile or two away across the city, they`d heard plenty and knew all about the families reputation for being rough and that they liked a drink when they`d finished work. They didn`t want her to

196

have anything to do with Granddad or the family. Granddad told me he had to work hard to win them round.

Dad remembered when he was about 6 or 7 standing on the top of a chimney with tears streaming down his face. Not because he was crying or scared, but because of the wind. He wasn't allowed to cry anyway. If he hit his thumb with a lump hammer or if he hurt himself and granddad ever saw any tears, he would bellow at him, "Pack that in, you`r`e an Akiens, you don't cry. Be `ard ya soft bastard, be `ard". It was because they needed to be. That was how granddad was bought up. Imagine being like that with your kids today. Dad never bought us up like that, thankfully, he just wanted to make us all laugh. When he was 7 or 8 he had to start wearing glasses. He didn`t mind too much when he was told he needed to wear them like a lot of kids would. He always told us a firework went off in his face. It was only when we were older he came clean and told us, that was just to stop us pissing about with bangers.

These are some of the jobs they had to look forward to in the spring of 1960, Dad would have been 18 at the time. Some of the companies mentioned for chimney repairs and fitting lightning conductors were Taylor, Taylor and Hobson, Willow Dye works, Burroughs and Smith, Nabisco Frears biscuits Wigston, Allard and Co Harrison road. Frears and Black wanted their clock tower pointing.

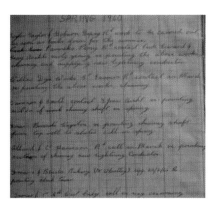

My Dads cousin recently told me a story id never heard before. He used to go along with my Dad and Granddad on some of the jobs they had to do. He wasn`t allowed to climb by his mam, great Aunt Gert, but he loved to go along and watch them working. One day they had a job on one of the factory chimneys on Frog island in Leicester. Granddad climbed the ladders to about 90 feet, then he stepped off the ladders and worked his way around the chimney, clinging on to the steel bands that held the old chimney together, so he could inspect the damage and what works needed to be carried out. He was using just his fingertips and toes as he went round the bands, they were probably less than an inch thick. It would`ve been one of the chimneys in the picture of frog island.

FROG ISLAND 1950`S

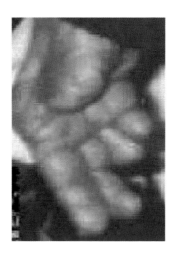

Only having the two fingers on his right hand would have made it a lot more dangerous. The strength you must need to go round the chimney on the bands like that, not to mention the balls needed. When he got down his trousers were burnt through inside his thighs and he had blisters running the length of his

198

legs. The fires were still lit on the boilers. Injuries like that were commonplace to them. This next one was written about another member of the family.

MR. AKIENS has had a number of narrow escapes from death and has smashed many a bone in his body, but that is part of the heritage to which he was born.

And if he had to live his life again, Mr. Akiens would run the same risks and break the same bones. The reason is plain — he was born into a family of steeplejacks, which prides itself as being second to none in the trade.

MR AKIENS has had a number of narrow escapes from death and has smashed many a bone in his body, but that is part of the heritage to which he was born. And if he had to live his life again, Mr. Akiens would run those same risks and break the same bones. The reason is plain – he was born into a family of steeplejacks, which prides themselves as being second to none in the trade.

****

They were often breaking bones, it was inevitable with all the demolition work they did. Sometimes dad and granddad worked on factories demolishing the top floors because they were perfectly comfortable working at height. They were called the top men. They`d knock the outer walls down brick by brick. They did very well out of these jobs, they could keep all the lead, electrical copper wiring, anything that could be salvaged that was worth salvaging. Dad used to burn the plastic off it in great big rolls, he never forgot the smell of it.

When they lived on Duchess street the kids used to play football in the road. There weren`t many cars about back then. They would often knock granddads door and tell him, "Mr Akiens, so and so`s taken the football off us cos it hit his window or car." Granddad would go marching straight round there and demand the "miserable bleeder" gave them the ball back.

Dad was the last generation of steeplejack in our branch the family. Born June 22nd 1942, a war baby. His name was LOL Akiens, short for Laurence. The funniest, cleverest, bravest man iv ever met, or ever likely to meet. Totally fearless, just like Granddad was. He had his faults but to me he was an amazing bloke. Times might have been hard and we may not have had everything we wanted, new bikes or designer trainers, but we were`n`t really bothered. We grew up having so many laughs. A few of my mates told me more than once, they wished their dads were like mine, always laughing and joking. He always gave me the best advice. One thing he told me quite often that I remember very well, is that "You have nothing to prove to anyone but yourself". No one does. I know just what he meant now.

His sense of humour was out of this world. He really was LOL by name and LOL by nature. If there was an opportunity to make someone laugh, or take the piss out of them, he took it. He certainly did with me over the years. He

200

was so quick witted, always acting the goat and winding people up. Anyone that knew him, knew his laugh.

Dad loved the work they did and couldn`t wait to get on the ladders every morning. He`d been doing the job since before he even started school. He left school at 14 to start the job proper, earning a wage. He earnt more than most of his mates because he was paid danger money. They often had crowds of local people and the factory workers watching them go about their business high above them.

Dad played up to them and put on a show up there. He played on the chimneys when he was a lad. He used to joke he had his own swing and no one else dared to play on it. He would be riding the seat probably pointing or painting the chimney or helping granddad fit a lightning conductor, with a crowd of people watching below. Sat on a 9" by 2 foot wooden plank suspended from a pulley by old, brown, creaky, very rough ropes either side of him. He would hold himself flat against the chimney wall and wait for a strong gust of wind to come along. Then he would kick himself off the wall into the wind, and it would blow him round the back of the chimney out of view. He could sometimes hear people below shouting and screaming, he thought that was funny. The factory workers thought he was mad, he was only a kid, playing. He often had sandwiches for lunch, a treat would be a lump of raw liver between two rounds of dry bread. He`d sit at the top of a chimney with one leg dangling down the inside of the chimney and one leg outside. I don't know what would make me throw up more, the sandwich or the height.

Dad gave some members of the family comical nicknames for a laugh, names that sounded good to him, or funny. My younger brother fell down a railway embankment and cut his shoulder badly on a broken milk bottle, he had 24 stiches. He got the nickname scarback Ako. My older brother had a horrific freak bike accident, he went over the handlebars after the front mud guard dropped into the wheel. He smashed his face on the road taking all the skin off one side of his face. He went along the road on his face for a couple of feet, until his head hit the kerb. The bike and his body flipped over snapping his neck. He had multiple skull fractures, broke his neck and died, for a couple of minutes in the hospital, but they managed to bring him back. He broke c4, the same bone Christopher Reeve the superman actor broke. The next day he sat picking out bits of broken teeth. It was a miracle seeing him walk down the hospital stairs the next day for a fag, with his neck in a brace. He got the nickname scarface Ako.

He gave me a few nicknames over the years. I was always climbing climbing something, trees, probably scrumping or just because I wanted to. I could climb onto the concrete shed at the side of our house when I was 4. Mrs Coote next door had an apple tree in her garden, we used to take running jumps into it off the shed, mam used to go mad. She said this was a familiar sight of me pictured below, my arse disappearing over a wall. This was taken down Martin Street in Belgrave. I used to get branches from the tree in the garden at the back of grandma and granddads house to make bow and arrows. Granddad gave us the string he used in the garden to tie things to canes.

I got a bit of a name in the family for getting into trouble, even at that very young age, I was a bit of a black sheep of the family. I couldn't wait to get to school and have a fight with someone. Dad told me it was ok if it was with someone bullying another kid. I often came home with a black eye or a fat lip, scraped knuckles, scuffed shoes and holes in my trousers. If I wasn't fighting or thieving, I was probably planning one or the other. I eventually stopped a lot of that, i preferred playing on the school roof to the playground. Its not exactly hard to see where I got that from. I used to find loads of tennis balls and footballs up there on Wolsey house school. Id swap them for things with the other kids, marbles or sweets or something. One of my best mates who liked to go up the drainpipes with me was a girl, a proper tom boy. We would be standing on the edge of Ellis school roof, looking down probably about 30 or 40 feet, and she would go to push me off, then grab my shoulder or sleeve to pull me back and say, "saved your life". One day she did it, and ripped the sleeve off my bomber jacket. Luckily we weren't on a school roof. I went head first about 5 or 6 feet down onto a pile of bricks from the path at the back of her house on Drummond road. I took a load of skin off my arm and forehead.

Her mam patched me up and sewed my sleeve back on. We were laughing about that on facebook not long ago.

The year dad passed away I had twins born on my birthday, Joel Thomas and Georgia Rae. He gave me another nickname, he called me Goldenballs Ako. I had to think for a few seconds at what he meant when he first called me it, then I got the joke. He was laughing as he said it. He always said laughter was the very best medicine you can have, and he meant it. Its got me through some extremely difficult times.

Dads brother my uncle, is the last steeplejack in our line that's still alive. He moved away to Rugby to start a family a year or two before Granddad and Dad wound up the business, because the work was so sporadic by the early 1970`s. He was always running marathons, breaking records, doing the family proud. He broke 24 club records over a thirty year period, 18 of them still stand. I know Dad was proud of his brother because of the grit and determination he must have needed to finish some of those gruelling races. Running past all those pubs for a start. Although one year when he ran the London Marathon, he actually stopped off in a pub half way round for a quick pint, then went on to finish the race. What an absolute legend. Dad gave him the nickname roadrunner Ako.

When most people retire, they take up golf or some other gentle hobby in their old age. Not my uncle. In this photo, he`s been retired a couple of years, aged about 67 or 68 !!! Photo courtesy of A Melbourne.

Me and Dad on my 21st Birthday.

He remembered looking down from chimneys during the 1950`s when there were still lots of them about. He would see other steeplejacks working on smaller, cleaner, less dangerous chimneys. He said it felt great that he was working on chimneys much bigger, dirtier and dangerous than theirs. He was just a young lad working on chimneys grown men weren`t brave enough to take on. He said they always looked down on other steeplejacks, in more ways than one. Dad was very proud that he wasn`t just a steeplejack, he was an Akiens steeplejack. That meant a lot to all of them, they were all very proud of that. They didn`t cherry pick their work. They took on every job they were ever asked to do, however dangerous.

Dad was told about several big chimneys in Derbyshire somewhere, before his time. Because of where they were situated, they got battered by very strong winds almost constantly. Only the family ever worked on them, the local steeplejacks in the area wouldn`t take them on because of how dangerous the work was.

Dad told me a story of when him and granddad were working on a chimney in the 1950`s I think, dad would be a teenager. It was an overcast day and it just started to rain. They wanted to get the job done that day so they could get paid and decided to stick it out. There were rumbles of thunder but they carried on. Then out of the darkening sky, a bolt of lightning struck the aluminium roof on the factory below them. Dad said the whole chimney stack shook beneath them. Granddad ordered Dad to make his way down to the van while he finished off. Then a few minutes later as dad reached the van, another bolt of lightning hit the same factory roof. Granddad finished the job and came down when he was good and ready. If there were a picture in the dictionary for the word stubborn, it would be granddads photo. No one ever told him what to do, whoever or whatever you were, except maybe Grandma. Dad used to say " We saw lightning from above that day, your granddad seen it twice. Not many people can say they`ve seen that ". He used to joke that after that first lightning strike hit the factory roof, Granddad probably stuck his two remaining victory fingers up at the heavens, and called someone up there a bastard.

When we were kids if we were watching the telly and it started to rain, Dad would take the Ariel out of the back of it. He was most insistent that we didn't plug it back in until he said we could. He knew only too well the damage a lightning strike could cause. He said it in that voice he had at times when you knew he meant what he said. He had a voice that made you freeze, similar to the one granddad had when he was pissed off. I know because I had a fight with my brother once and granddad heard about it. He went berserk at me.

Iv spent a good few years researching and compiling this tiny slice of England and Leicester history. Its only now during the lockdown of this covid pandemic, that iv actually got my finger out to make it into an actual book. Im glad i listened to all those stories the older people in the family told me. Personally, i think its important our children`s children and so on, know where they come from. Even though they will never know us. We all have valuable histories to pass on to our families. Once those histories are forgotten, they are gone for good. If we don`t write or record our histories of who we are and where we come from, we will all end up just a forgotten name on a headstone somewhere, within a few generations. Like all those people on the millions of headstones everywhere.

Two factory workers got chatting to Dad when he was working on their chimney one day. One of them asked him " How do you get the ladders all the way up there ?" The other bloke cut in before Dad had a chance to speak and said, "That`s easy, they just hoist them up by rope from that pulley at the top". Dad agreed with him with a straight face, and said "Yeah that`s right, but its a bit tricky, trying to thread the rope through that pulley, from all the way down here !"

205

When dad was about 20, he went in town on the lash with his mates to the Palais on Humberstone gate. At the end of the night they were walking back past the new Tesco multi storey car park on Lee circle, pictured below. Dad climbed to the top of it on the outside, walked all the way round it on the edge, and then climbed back down. Granddad read him the riot act over it. He knew how stupid he`d been showing off like that when he was drunk.

When I was 15 Dad got the job of pointing the house, the ridge tiles and the chimney, for the people who owned the Tudor Rose chip van. They lived on Abbey lane near Rons cafe. He`d worked for them before, they thought a lot of Dad. When they sold the van they took over the chippy in Rothley. I went in there a couple of years after Dad passed away, I was the pool team captain for Dads cousin Gordon Akiens at the Old Crown round the corner. They were gutted to hear the news, you could see it in their faces. A few people had the same look when I had to tell them. He made people laugh and he was great to be around. He asked me to help him on this job, it was the first time I worked with him. We nipped in Granddads on Beaumanor road to pick up the ladders we needed. There was a great big pile of them left over from the steeplejack days. There must have been 50 or more stacked up higher than the fence. As we got to the back gate of the house we were going to work on, Dad said, here we are, in you go. I was looking forward to cracking on with the job and earning a few quid. Just as I walked in the gateway, I felt a shove in the middle of my back, then i heard the gate slam shut behind me. The next thing, two pointer type dogs came bounding down the garden barking at me. Sheer panic kicked in. I said out loud purely by reaction, " F*****ell Dad, theyve got dogs ". But all I could hear was Dad laughing out loud. He was doubled up on the other side of the gate banging his hand on it. It was the first time I`d said the F word in front of him, and I didn't get bolloked for it.

206

He`d met the dogs before and knew they only barked, he knew I`d be ok. That was just his warped sense of humour, as grandma called it. You never knew when a wind up was coming with Dad. It was funny, we both laughed about it for most of that first day.

I had to rack out all the cement between the bricks up to about 15 feet high and mix all the compo for the both of us. Dad wouldn't let me go any higher up the ladders. He was very insistent on that point. He did all the work above that. I was busy pointing up some of the brickwork when dad shouted down to make sure I had plenty mixed. When I looked up my heart was in my mouth, I couldn't believe what I was seeing. He was just standing on the top of the chimney pots, reading the paper. He was just showing off.

When we were little, every Sunday morning dad would take us down grandma and granddads to their terraced house on Martin street in Belgrave. We`d walk down corporation road past the old Abbey pumping station. He told us Dracula lived there. He wasn`t trying to frighten us, that was just his sense of humour, we thought it was hilarious. To us kids it looked the sort of place where Dracula would live, when we walked past, coming home from the club on Saturday nights when it was dark.

Then we`d go across Holden street bridge, down Ross walk and over the park, Cossington street Reccy. On one of these visits to Martin street, i was 3. Dad stood me on the dining table, and said "Can you sing Tom Jones for me". So i started singing Deliah or whatever song he`d been teaching me. Dad said, that`s lovely Scott, but i can`t hear you very well. Can you sing a bit louder? So i did. Then he said, yes that`s very good, but i still can`t hear you very well mate, can you sing it a bit louder.

So again i upped the volume. Again dad still couldn't hear me very well. In the end id be belting it out at the absolute top of my voice, lungs nearly bursting, sweat running down my forehead, with a face redder than one of granddads tomatoes. Dad would be in stitches laughing at me. Grandma would say, "Pack it in Lol, he`ll end up as warped as you if you carry on like that you silly bleeder." That was a story dad told loads of people over the years.

There was another game he liked playing where he went deaf. He would be laying on the carpet in front of the fire reading a book, and we would sit next to him to get warm. Suddenly, he`d grab us and pin us to the floor. He would tickle us until we said sorry, or submit. Every time we said it, he said he couldn't hear us. If you've ever been tickled until you can`t` take it anymore, then tickled some more, and then some more, you`ll know what I mean. It was like funny torture. If ever there was such a thing as a laughter Barrier, dad broke it when he was playing with us.

I had earache quite a lot when I was a kid. Mam would get the ear drops and dad would tell me to lay on the settee with my head on a cushion. He told me by the time it dripped out of my other ear onto the cushion, that's when the earache would go. Id be there for hours, long after the earache had gone, still checking the cushion every so often to see if the drops had gone through to it.

Dad used to enjoy doing jigsaw puzzles, he would spend days , weeks even doing a thousand piece one. He had a 3 x 2 sheet of plywood that he would slide under the settee. I would often sit for a couple of hours helping him. When it was finished, he would call me in to show me and say, "Can you believe that, all that time doing it, and theres one sodding piece missing". At which point, id produce the piece from my pocket and pop it in place. Then id dash out of the room, with dad laughing, shouting after me, "You little shit, you`ve done the bleeder again." He always got me back somehow though.

When I was 14 I came off my bike and smashed my face on the kerb chipping a front tooth. I had an inch long scab on my top lip for weeks. When I was out in the street playing with my mates, dad would come along, goose stepping up the street . He`d shout over to me, "ayyup adolf, hows it goin". It was funny looking back, but embarrassing at the time in front of all your mates. He found something funny in just about everything.

I remember coming home from work one day feeling a bit extra knackered. I thought i`d go and have a kip to catch up on a bit of sleep. The next thing I remembered was dad waking me up. "Come on Scott its quarter to eight, you`re going to be late for work." Shit ! Im supposed to start at 6. So I dived out of bed in a panic, rushing round getting dressed, quick wash and brush my teeth. Then 5 minutes in front of the fire with a fag and a cup of tea to wake up. As im sat there slowly coming round, it started to dawn on me. I thought to myself, "How come everyones up, and they`re watching coronation street". I`d only been in bed an hour. Dad found that hilarious.

My dad, granddad and my uncle were demolishing a 90 foot chimney one day that was so rotten, they could see daylight coming through the brick work. Granddad told both of them only he was going up this one. He sent them into the factory to make sure all the workers were at the other end of the factory, just in case. Granddad prised a big concrete block off the top of the chimney using a long crow bar, with the intention of dropping it down the inside. But one side of the chimney collapsed and it pivoted off the top and came down the outside of the chimney. It went straight through the factory roof with a very loud bang. Plumes of dust filled the area. All the workers came out a minute later coughing and spluttering, plastered in dust and debris. Dad and my uncle thought it was hilarious at the time, granddad probably didn`t though.

The factory owners allowed them to fall into the kind of states like this one above, a modern photo of a chimney that's been abandoned. The family actually climbed chimneys like these, in this sort of state. And this one looks like a baby to me. You couldn't blame the other steeplejacks for walking away. But the family never did.

A bloke asked dad once, what would he do if the chimney fell while they were working on it. Dad said, "Well its simple, if the chimney falls over, you just run like the clappers down it as its falling and jump off at the bottom."

The thing with dad was, he said everything with such a straight face. People never knew when to take him seriously, until he started laughing. He often said , " If you can say something with a really straight face, you can make people believe almost anything".

It would be the worst nightmare for the vast majority of people, having to climb to those dizzy heights. The fear of heights Agrophobia, is the world's number one fear. Dad lost count of how many people that had said to him, "You wouldn`t get me up there, not for anything." He said he wished he had a quid for every time someone said it to him.

Dad never had much time for the church, religion or bible bashers in general. He believed in God but not through any religion. In his opinion religion has caused more wars and divide than anything. It was blatantly obvious how much time he had for religion whenever any Jehovah`s witness`s turned up at the front door. He loved winding them up. He`d chat with them for a good 15 minutes, asking them awkward questions about the bible, just to see what bullshit they came out with. Then he liked to finish off with one last Question. "Can I ask you something i`d really love to know". He`d have their full attention by this point, it must have been unusual finding someone so willing to speak to them round where we lived. He`d say " Can you please tell me, why a couple of smart, good looking, intelligent young people like yourselves, are going round bothering decent hard working people at home, with all this claptrap?" Then he`d slam the door in their shell shocked faces. They were lucky if he didn't chuck in "Piss off and don't come back" as he did it. His dislike for any religion probably stemmed from some of his experiences working for the churches. Like this incident he remembered from when he was a young lad.

This is one story he told me that he found especially funny. When he was about 6 or 7, he was working on a church steeple with Granddad. The vicar moaned that it took dad too long to climb down for a toilet break, and he didn't like him trudging dust and muck through the place. He was only a little boy, with a little boys bladder. When he needed to go, he needed to go. So, after that rollocking dad didn't bother climbing all the way back down again. Instead of risking another telling off from the vicar, he just wrote his name on the church roof, in great big letters.

He said " Well, It wasn't like the vicar would ever see it, he wasn't brave enough to go up there". He might have had a little boys bladder, but he had bigger balls than that vicar had.

Granddads business finally folded for him and dad in the mid 1970's, there wasn't enough work around for them anymore. Another few more years and that would have been my job. Newer, cleaner forms of energy had came along and the chimneys were disappearing. Steeplejacks weren't needed like they used to be. They would go weeks without any work at all. Granddad retired and the job basically died, so they jacked it all in. It didn't help when some thieving bastard broke into his van on Beaumanor road and stole all his tools. Dad had a young family to feed and Mam didn't want him taking those risks anymore, so he went to college and learnt bricklaying. Some of his cousins and uncles carried on for a few more years but eventually everyone called it a day.

For details of how to get your signed 1st edition hard back copy of this book, please email

enquiries@the-akiens-steeplejacks.com

Or you can buy it online on the Waterstones, Amazon uk, or WH Smiths websites using the ISBN NUMBER: 9781527272811